The best gymnast the world has ever seen

Here and on the cover, Simone Biles wears GUCCI, photographed by
Alasdair McLellan and styled by Jonathan Kaye.

The Gentlewoman
Issue n° 16
Autumn & Winter 2017

Hello there.

DIOR

ST

Fashion is about the everyday and the every...
the political stage of our freedoms. For the ...
show we have decided to look at the role that w...
in the shaping of modern society, their p...
participation and social achievements. It is no...
of convenience, it is a demand of the current m...

SO

Thursday
February 23rd
at 6:00 pm
Via Fogazzaro 36
Milano

PRADA

PRADA

+44 207 399 2030 PRADA.COM

SERIES 7 PHOTOGRAPHED BY
BRUCE WEBER

LOUIS VUITTON

SERIES 7 PHOTOGRAPHED BY
BRUCE WEBER

LOUIS VUITTON

GUCCI

GUCCI

SAINT LAURENT

SAINT LAURENT

PRESERVATION HALL AND OTHER STORIES

NEW ORLEANS, LOUISIANA
MAY 11-13 2017
BY ALASDAIR McLELLAN

miu miu

+44 207-399 2030 MIUMIU.COM

PRESERVATION HALL AND OTHER STORIES

NEW ORLEANS, LOUISIANA
MAY 11-13 2017
BY ALASDAIR MCLELLAN

miu miu

GIORGIO ARMANI

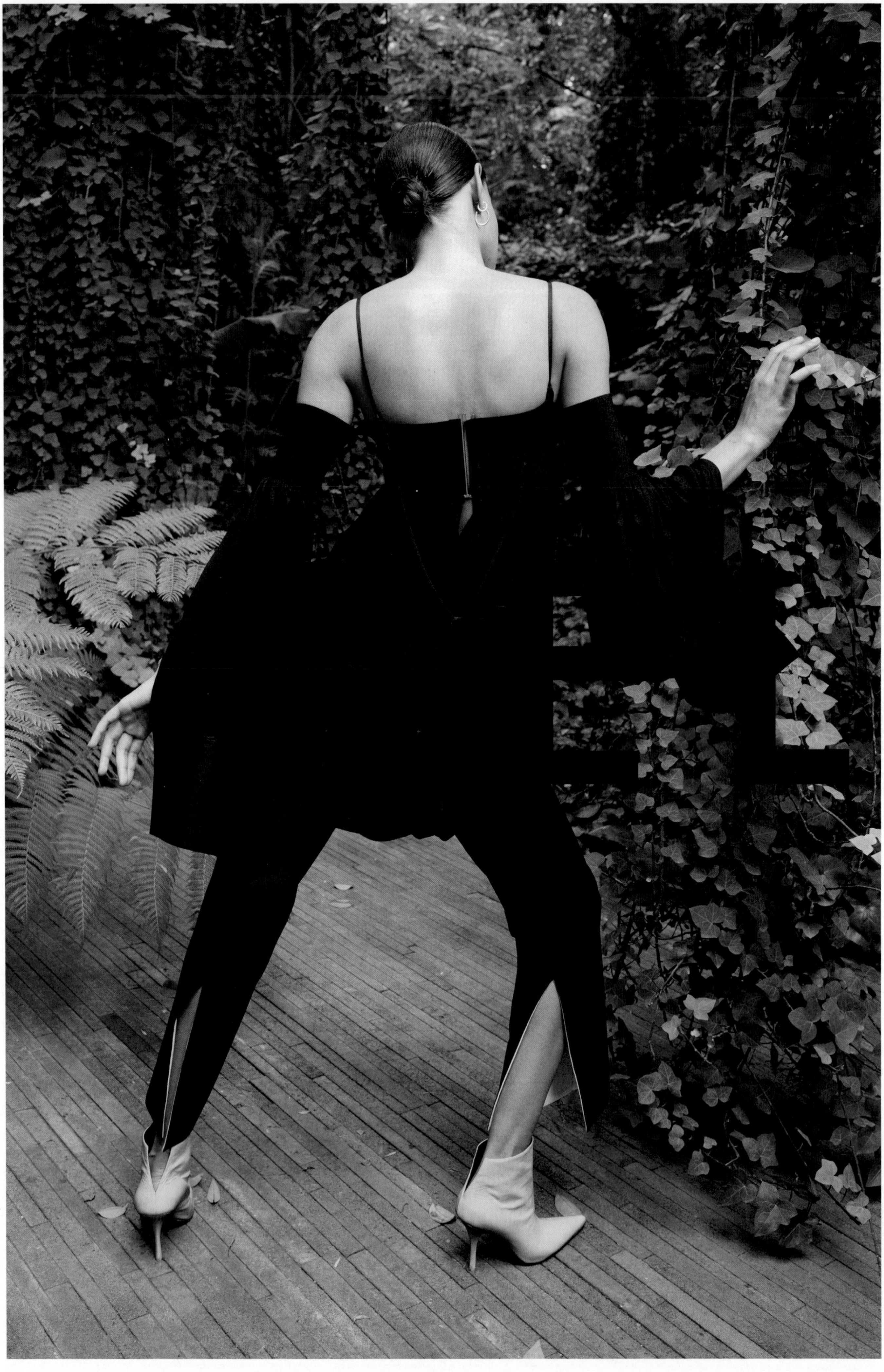

Billboard artwork: Andy Warhol, *Elvis 11 Times (Studio Type)*, 1963 © The Andy Warhol Foundation / ARS, photographed at The Andy Warhol Museum, Pittsburgh
205 Calvin Klein Jeans patch: Photo, Richard Avedon® © 2017 The Richard Avedon Foundation
CALVIN KLEIN 205W39NYC Fall 2017: photographed May 2017, Mojave Desert, California

CALVIN KLEIN
205 W39 NYC

128 Mount Street
lanvin.com

LANVIN

PARIS

SONIA RYKIEL PARIS

SONIA RYKIEL PARIS

STELLA McCARTNEY

STELLAMCCARTNEY.COM

DSQUARED2

Angok and Cara, Midtown, New York

DVF

dvf.com

DIANE VON
FURSTENBERG

sacai

KENZO PARIS

KENZO – La Collection Memento welcomes back to life pieces that are truly KENZO, created during Kenzo Takada's journey and Carol Lim and Humberto Leon first years at the house. For the first outing in this series of collections, photographer Hans Feurer went back to Lanzarote,

CHRISTOPHER KANE

THE FIRST FRAGRANCE FOR HER

JASON WU

SPORTMAX

SPORTMAX

MSGM

JOSEPH

EST 1887

SMYTHSON

OF BOND STREET

WATCH THE FILM AT SMYTHSON.COM

BY APPOINTMENT TO
HER MAJESTY THE QUEEN
GOLDSMITHS & SILVERSMITHS
WILLIAM & SON
LONDON

WILLIAM & SON

LONDON

34 – 36 BRUTON STREET   LONDON   W1J 6QX   020 7493 8385   WILLIAMANDSON.COM

STUART WEITZMAN

ROKSANDA

ERIKA CAVALLINI

rucoline.com

RUCOLINE

MILANO FIRENZE ROMA DUBAI TOKYO BEIJING SHANGHAI SHENZHEN HONG KONG

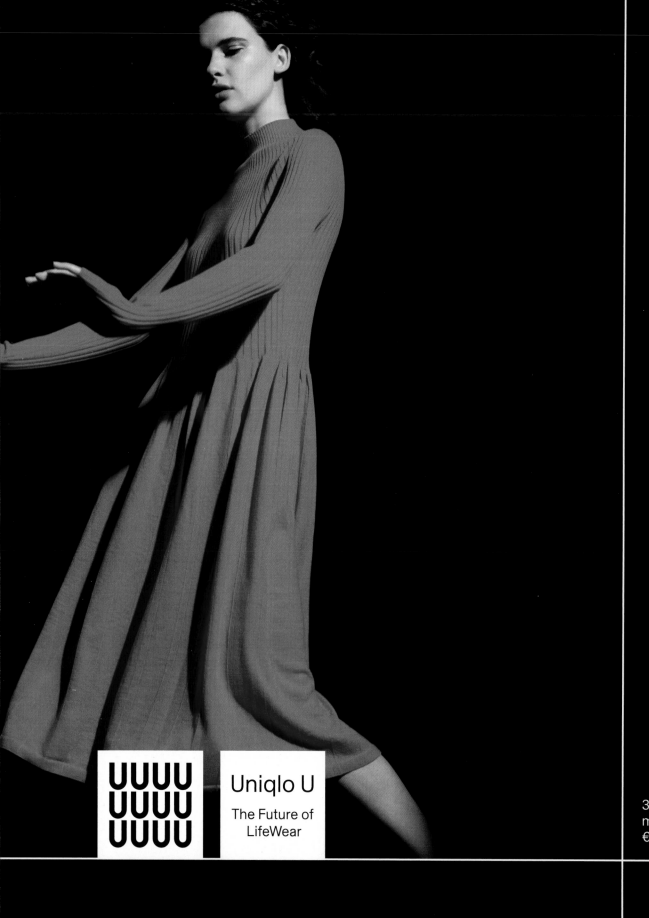

Uniqlo U
The Future of
LifeWear

3D merino ribbed
mock neck dress
€ 59.90

Uniqlo U
Always experimenting.
Always evolving.

BY MALENE BIRGER

the gentlewoman

Issue n° 16
Autumn & Winter 2017

Simone Biles on greatness: see pages 210 to 223.
Photographed by Alasdair McLellan, styled by Jonathan Kaye.

....

The Gentlewoman
73–75 Kenton Street
London WC1N 1NN
United Kingdom
Phone +44 20 8616 5433
office@thegentlewoman.com
thegentlewoman.com

....

Editor in Chief: Penny Martin
Creative Director: Jop van Bennekom
Fashion Director: Jonathan Kaye
Art Direction and Design: Veronica Ditting
Publisher: Rebecca Morris
Associate Editors: Kathryn Holliday, Gert Jonkers
Senior Editor: Richard O'Mahony
Advertising Director: Elizabeth Sims
Production Editor: Jordan Kelly
Designers: Florine Bonaventure, Franca Moor, Studio Veronica Ditting
Editorial Assistant: Lucy Milligan
Website Design: Studio Scasascia
Office Manager: Kirsten Abildgaard
Sub-Editor: Laura Martz

....

Contributing Editors
Sophie Elmhirst, Seb Emina, Ann Friedman, Cristina Ruiz, Susie Rushton

....

Contributing Fashion Editors
Francesca Burns, Alex Harrington, Jane How, Max Pearmain

....

Contributing Writers
Joan Juliet Buck, Kate Finnigan, Susan Irvine, Marina O'Loughlin, Deborah Orr,
Horacio Silva, Mark Smith, Andrew Tucker

....

Contributing Photographers
Clara Balzary, Blommers/Schumm, Colin Dodgson, Zoë Ghertner,
Chloé Le Drezen, Alasdair McLellan, Oliver Hadlee Pearch, Katja Rahlwes,
Chris Rhodes, Karim Sadli, Nigel Shafran, Theo Sion, Andrea Spotorno,
Bruno Staub, Jack Webb, Harley Weir, Paul Wetherell

(continued on page 82)

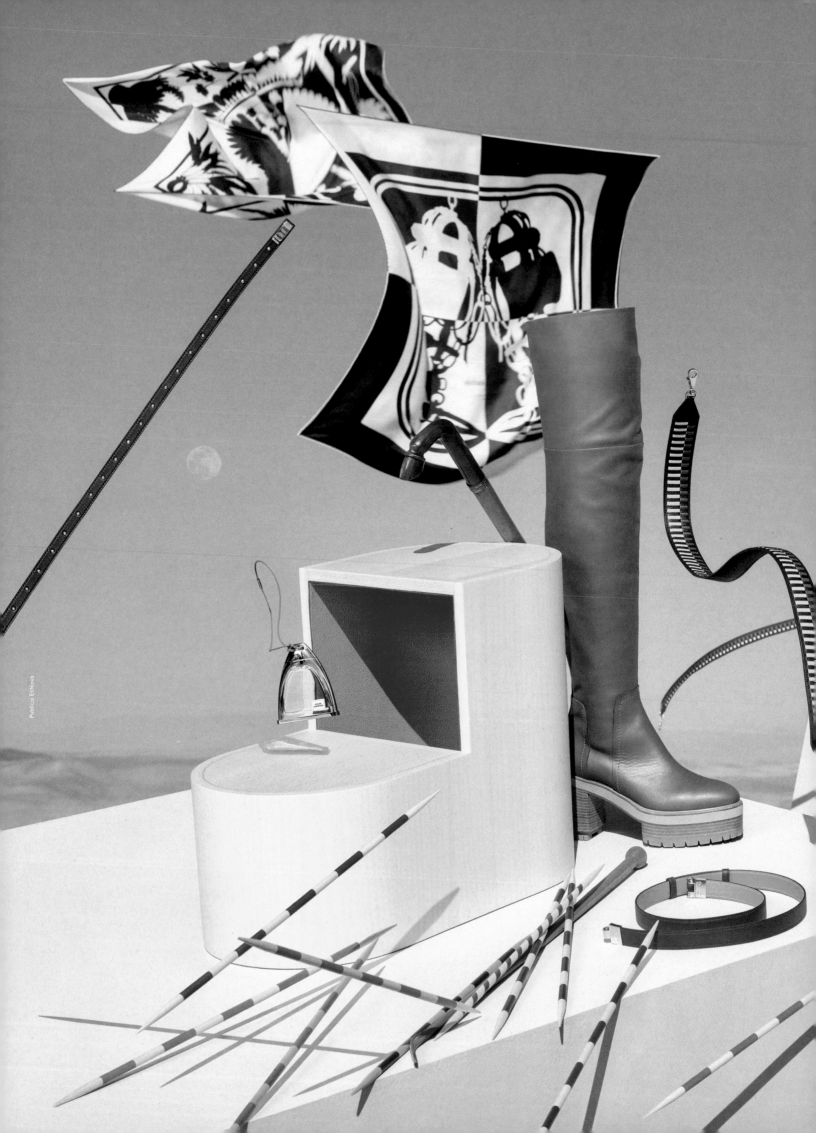

OBJECTS COME ALIVE

HERMÈS
PARIS

The Gentlewoman
Issue n° 16
Autumn & Winter 2017

Masthead, continued

....

Contributing Stylists, Artists and Producers
Akki, Art Partner, Suzanne Beirne, Bird Production, Boals Artists, Alexander Bock,
Damien Boissinot, Brachfeld Paris, Joey Choy, Max Clark, Christelle Cocquet,
Eliza Conlon, Connect the Dots, Francelle Daly, Thomas de Kluyver, Elsa Durrens,
Gina Edward, Ramona Eschbach, Sandy Ganzer, Malina Gilchrist, Georgina Graham,
Cyndia Harvey, Luke Hersheson, Adam Hindle, Staci-Lee Hindley, Fara Homidi,
Alexandra Jachno, Emilie Kareh, Laura Holmes Production, Jenny Longworth,
Didier Malige, Matt Mulhall, Mari Ohashi, Samuel Paul, Nigel Peake, Mike Pocock,
Pony Projects, Anthony Preel, Nikki Providence, Ama Quashie, Niamh Quinn,
Rep Limited, Jason Rider, Rosco Production, Tamara Rothstein, Gerard Santos,
Carole Savaton, Samuel Ellis Scheinman, Noah Shelley, Gemma Smith Edhouse,
Kei Terada, Nafisa Tosh, Hiromi Ueda, Spencer Vrooman, Webber Represents

....

Thank You
Ace Hotel (New York), Magnus Åkesson, Iranzu Baker, Karl-Johan Bogefors,
The Collective Shift, Charlotte Cotton, Ann Friedman, Lucy Glyn, Karin Gustafsson,
Jane Kersel, Matthew Moneypenny, Brian Phillips, Jo Taylor, Ellis Woodman,
Linsey Young

....

Advertising Enquiries

UK and Europe
Elizabeth Sims at The Gentlewoman
elizabeth@thegentlewoman.com, Phone +44 20 7242 8802, Mobile +44 7922 220074

Italy
Fabio Montobbio at Rock Media
fabio@rockmedia.it, Phone +39 0278 2608, Mobile +39 3496 195880

USA
Michael Bullock
michael@fantasticman.com, Phone +1 917 349 0417

....

Published by
Fantastic Woman Ltd., London

International Distribution
MMS Ltd
info@mmslondon.co.uk, Phone +44 1992 676064, mmslondon.co.uk

Subscription Service
Bruil & Van De Staaij
bruil.info

....

....

Architectural Tour

 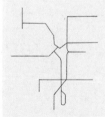

Allow us, together with our friends at COS, to take you on an architectural exploration
of London and Los Angeles. Experience a century of the modernist dream in each
city — fulfilled and unfulfilled — with the map enclosed in this issue as your informative
companion.

thegentlewoman.com/club

....

Drawings by Nigel Peake

ALEXANDER M^CQUEEN

The Gentlewoman
Issue n° 16
Autumn & Winter 2017

Part One: ....
....

The Australian model Charlee Fraser travelled to the shoreline of Nice to try on black leather looks on pages 127-133. Here, she's in a policeman jacket with metallic appliqué by CALVIN KLEIN 205W39NYC. ....
....

First take.

BURBERRY

BURBERRY

The Gentlewoman
Issue n° 16
Autumn & Winter 2017

Encounters.

Denim looks worth lining up for: pages 186–193. Vintage black denim jacket by MARL-BORO CLASSICS and vintage check-denim bondage trousers from CONTEMPORARY WARDROBE. Blue denim boots by DRIES VAN NOTEN, blue Trotteur bag by CÉLINE. ...

NORTHAMPTON, ENGLAND

Church's

English shoes

The Gentlewoman
Issue n° 16
Autumn & Winter 2017

Part Three: ....

A high-visibility-fabric ballgown, £22.99, from TRAID: one of 14 outfits assembled by the stylist Jane How for under £41.96, photographed by Harley Weir on pages 270–283. ..

Exhibitionism.

Chloé

KVADRAT / RAF SIMONS

FOR SUPERWOMEN™

©2017 FitFlop Ltd

UMA THURMAN | FITFLOP.COM

j-w-anderson.com

JWANDERSON

The commitment to
continually make work
under any circumstances
is the practice.

LORNA SIMPSON ARTIST REPRESENTED BY

HAUSER & WIRTH

shot by scheltens & abbenes

12 rue cambon, paris

paco rabanne

The Gentlewoman
Issue n° 16
Autumn & Winter 2017

First take.

Modern Meaning

The shimmering melodies of Amber Arcades are the work of the multi-instrumentalist singer-songwriter whose real name is Annelotte de Graaf. When she stepped on to the indie music stage last year with her flawless debut album, *Fading Lines*, the 28-year-old was still working as a legal aide to Syrian refugees for the Dutch Immigration and Naturalisation Service (IND), having previously sat on a United Nations war crimes tribunal. Life's a mix of light and shade for Annelotte, who grew up listening to Abba in a Utrecht co-op. It's taught her that altruism can be its own reward.

Interview
Richard O'Mahony

Portraits
Katja Rahlwes

→

Here and on page 106, Annelotte wears a white silk pussy-bow blouse by 3.1 PHILLIP LIM and vintage jeans by LEVI'S. Overleaf, she also wears rose-gold La Linge C rings by REPOSSI.

Richard: I'm not sure whether I should call you Amber or Annelotte — which do you prefer?

Annelotte: Call me Annelotte. Amber Arcades is my stage name. There was no way I could use my own; it's just too tricky to pronounce. Especially my surname, De Graaf — it's got that Dutch, back-of-the-throat, guttural sound going on. I'd actually prefer to perform under my real name, but I understand that Amber Arcades works better.

R: So where does it come from?

A: I used to wear an amber necklace as a child. I was a bit of dreamer and had a difficult time interacting with the other kids at school, so my parents had a homeopathic doctor examine me — they were very into alternative medicine and New Age things like crystal healing and stones. The doctor said I should wear an amber stone around my neck; apparently, it would help me to be more grounded and engaged with my environment. I'm not sure it worked, but it did give me my stage name.

R: What does an alias do for you as a performer?

A: It's not like I've cultivated a stage persona, like Lady Gaga. I can see the benefits of having that clearly defined character and sound, though, and how it makes business sense to be categorised easily. But that calculated identity's not for me. Some days I might be in the mood to write a grungy rock song, other days something more dreamy and folky. If I had to write a record with only one kind of sound, I think I'd lose inspiration in a day.

R: What kind of music did you listen to when you were growing up?

A: Do you remember that band A-Teens?

R: The teenage Abba tribute group from Sweden? Of course!

A: Yes! I think their album was my first record. My mother bought it for me when I was 11 — she was always playing Abba when I was a kid. Then as a teenager I was a goth and was really into

Annelotte de Graaf

Annelotte de Graaf

"At the IND I worked with refugees and asylum seekers; it almost feels selfish to be a musician."

this Finnish symphonic metal band called Nightwish — have you heard of them? The lead singer is a woman, and she was just awesome to me as a 15-year-old. I think my own music lies somewhere in between those references.

R: It's only within the last year that you've been working full-time as a musician, right?

A: Yes, I quit my job as an immigration lawyer with the IND last September. Touring and working full-time just became too much for me. It was Monday to Thursday in the office, then on Friday my band and I would drive from the Netherlands to the United Kingdom to perform, drive back on Sunday night, and then I was back in the IND offices in Hoofddorp again on Monday morning. I had zero free time. I didn't see any friends or family and had little opportunity to write music — something had to give.

R: How did you feel about making the break?

A: Scared shitless! Giving up the security of a full-time job was terrifying — would I be able to manage financially? I wasn't earning that much money from music yet, and I'd spent my savings on making the first album. Change is something I can find a bit overwhelming, but I know it's necessary for me to push myself because I want to experience so much of what life has to offer. I feel much more in control now, scheduling my day so that I'm getting everything I want in there: writing music, cooking, yoga, seeing my granny. She's 83.

R: Is the music industry everything you imagined it would be?

A: It's not as glamorous. But there have been moments. Last year I was nominated for an Edison award, which is like the Dutch Grammys, and the ceremony was good fun. There was a free bar, and everyone was dressed in designer clothes. I think I wore a €30 black jumpsuit I'd bought that day.

R: How rock 'n' roll!

A: No — how Dutch! We have an expression in the Netherlands: Just act normal and then you're strange enough. I'm not an extravagant person, and I'm not really into having fun. I mean, I like to have a good time — I'll have a drink now

and again, nothing crazy — but having fun isn't my main priority in life.

R: That seems so at odds with the psychedelic, fantastical pleasure of your music.

A: That mindset helps to keep me focused, and that's especially important in this business. As a musician, your work is never finished. Theoretically, I can be productive at any time. I could be writing right now. And sometimes I get anxious when I'm not. Even if I've written 16 songs, why not 20? Maybe the four I didn't write would be better. And that can be tiring.

R: You recorded and mixed your first album in nine days, is that right?

A: That was more about circumstance — it was the only studio time I could afford! I'd used all of my savings, €12,000, and sold an old banjo and a mandolin, so the stakes were high.

R: What did your colleagues make of your career change?

A: They thought I was a badass for pursuing something so uncertain. They'd been so supportive, taking on some of my cases while I was off on tour, but I couldn't keep expecting them to facilitate that. I didn't want to become a difficult employee who was always asking for time off; I wanted to leave with some goodwill behind me. Maybe someday I will want to go back there, you know?

R: You could return to your old job if you wanted?

A: At the moment it feels like the right time to be doing what I'm doing. I'm 28, I love making music, I enjoy all the travelling, I don't have children. But who knows — maybe in 10 years' time I'll crave something more stable again. One of the most satisfying things about working with the IND was feeling like I was actually helping people and contributing to a greater good, if that doesn't sound too worthy! In a way, it almost feels a bit selfish to be a musician.

R: But surely by making music that people enjoy you're contributing to people's happiness in some way?

A: Sure, but with law it seemed clearer: someone would come to me with a problem, and here's how I could help resolve it. I was working with refugees

and asylum seekers from countries like Syria, Eritrea and Somalia, guiding them through the whole process, building and reviewing their cases before a final decision on their application. And these were vulnerable people who'd arrived in a new country not knowing the legal system or their rights, nowhere to live, no money, no anything.

R: I can see how the inner workings of the music industry might seem somewhat less honourable at times.

A: It can be hard to know if I am making a specific difference. Yes, people buy the records; yes, they come to my shows, tell me how much they're enjoying the music. And it's humbling to affect people in such a direct and personal way. But there are so many other talented musicians out there doing amazing work that if I didn't make music, people would just listen to those other artists instead.

A★TEENS

The A-Teens originally formed as Abba Teens in 1988 but abbreviated their name at the request of Benny Andersson and Björn Ulvaeus.

Styling: Eliza Conlon. Hair: Kei Terada at Julian Watson Agency. Make-up: Georgina Graham at Management + Artists. Manicure: Jenny Longworth at CLM. Set design: Suzanne Beirne at D+V Management. Photographic assistance: Liberto Fillo. Styling assistance: Annabelle Peacock. Make-up assistance: Kat Ali. Set design assistance: Abbey Pearson.

There are moments (and this is one) when the prevailing mood ought not to be understood purely via the material world. These are times when emotion and sensation are more representative proxies for the modern state of being — a receptiveness to experience that is the true luxury of our era.

Open up and give yourself over to:
Devotion
Excess
Entrainment
Anonymity
Surrender
and
Fascination (four times)

Modern States and 4 Fascinations

LA FEMME
PRADA

MILANO

DAL 1913

INTENSE

THE NEW FRAGRANCE

#pradaintense

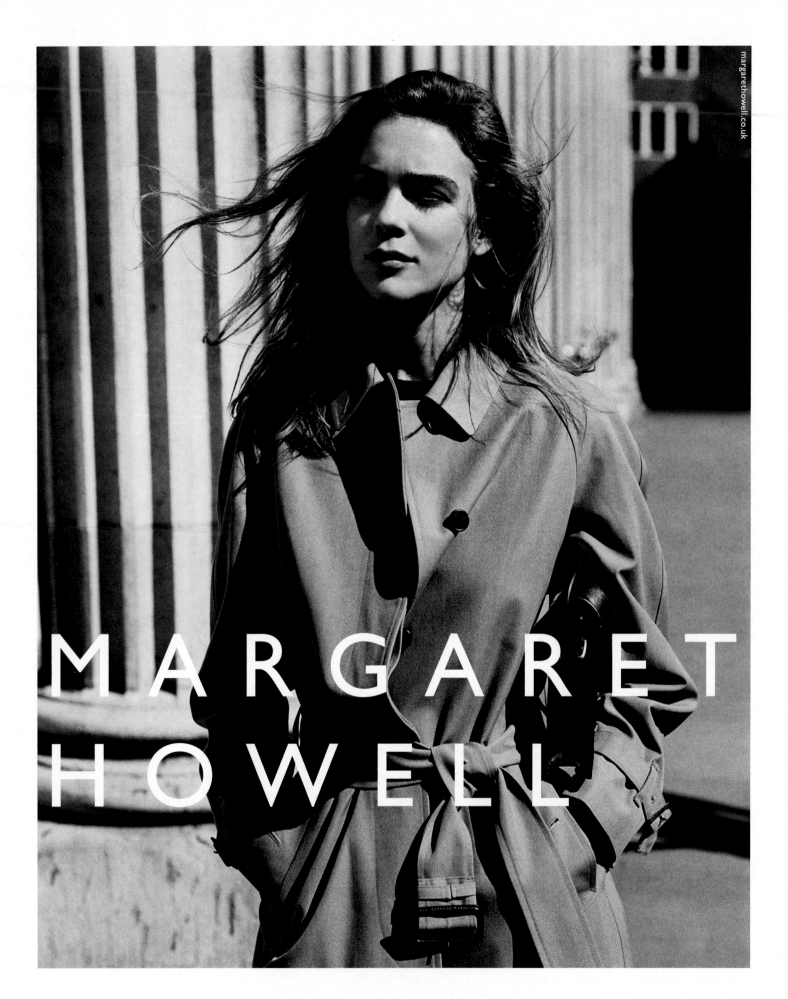

MARGARET HOWELL

By Susan Irvine

I was devoted to orris before I knew what it was, or even *that* it was; I mean, before I knew that it was a thing in itself. And in a way orris is not a thing in itself, because one of its cardinal qualities is its capacity to harmonise the elements in a fragrance. It gives those other elements somewhere to live and breathe, but not just any old where. Orris gives a fragrance a sort of cloud architecture, as in an opium dream. It is deep, suave and radiant. When it comes to fragrance, it is It.

And yet all it actually is is the root – or rather rhizome – of the iris, the finest absolute being obtained from *Iris pallida*. Sometimes you see "iris" listed in a scent's ingredients rather than "orris", but it is still the root, matured over a number of years. Should you ever get hold of a lump of the stuff, it will smell earthy, maybe a bit carroty, with a vibration of violets. Some types have a buttery quality, others are powdery. Some are, impossibly, both. Orris is not sexy as we know sexy. Its sensuality is from another century. There's a soft modelling to it, like the flesh of the "Mona Lisa". For me, that painting is the visual corollary of orris: the quality of her skin, glowing, melting; the combination of golden tones and remote powdery blues.

You rarely get the full effect of orris now. You are more likely to come across a tantalising drop, as in Jason Wu's fragrance, where you have to wait for a hint to emerge from aqueous florals; or else sense it through a glass darkly, as in Twisted Iris from The Perfumer's Story, where fig, cedar and aldehydes play against it in a very sensual way.

If you want to hear the call of orris clearly, start with Chanel No 19. Those green chypres of the 1970s got their powdery quality from orris. I am devoted to them all, from the original version of Coriandre by Jean Couturier through No 19 to Clinique's Aromatics Elixir. They are cool and cryptic, tingling with crystalline powders, more of a Rive Gauche, woman-in-a-man's-suit thing than the "Mona Lisa". My orris obsession probably began here, since I was wearing Coriandre when I had my first kiss.

For orris's unctuous side, you have to seek out scents almost no one knows, such as Tiempe Passate by Antonia's Flowers or

Orris Noir by Ormonde Jayne, which is a kind of velvet smoke. There's a grisaille to orris, reflected in the names of fragrances such as Iris Silver Mist by Serge Lutens, and Orris Noir leans to this crepuscular side.

The greatest orris fragrance of them all, Iris Gris ("grey iris") by Jacques Fath, had this timbre to it, too. Launched in 1946, it disappeared a few years later. A perfumer of the old school gave me some more than 20 years ago. It came in a lab bottle with "Iris Gris" typed onto a scrap of paper and sellotaped to the side. How he came to be in possession of it is best left unsaid. The flacon lives at the back of my fridge, and from time to time I take it out and sniff it till I am intoxicated. I'm wearing a drop now because I'm writing about it, and I feel I am dissolving in a violet pool.

Photography by Chloé Le Drezen.

Devotion.

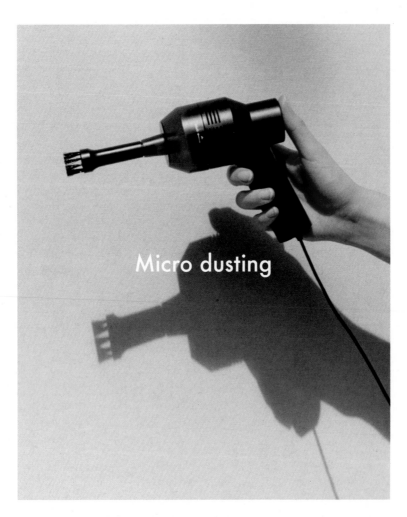

Micro dusting

There is satisfaction in discovering applications for a tool that are not strictly within its purview. Case in point: the handheld mini vacuum of the type used for cleaning computer keyboards, pictured here, is equally adept at banishing dust from the niggling corners of home libraries and the fragile pages of antiquarian books. Isn't the joy of book collecting partly in their care and display? And while a professional librarian's device, such as the mighty Pulvisina, used by institutions like the Bodleian Library, is out of the question for the average bibliophile, this miniature fellow does the job very nicely. As it also does with fancy apparel, deftly removing the micro particles that tend to accumulate in the fine webbing of Balenciaga's handsome Triple S trainers, for example. It's the little things.

USB mini vacuum cleaner computer keyboard brush dust handheld clean kit from AMAZON. Photography by Chloé Le Drezen.

A.P.C.

APC.FR

By Joan Juliet Buck

On assignment in Moscow a few years ago, I had dinner with my friend Owen in a restaurant jammed with bevelled glass screens and mahogany panels. The waiters were heavily costumed, and my handbag was given a miniature chair of its own. My first course was a mousse of smoked trout so delicate, so unusual, that I had barely finished it before I asked the waiter, who looked like an extra in *Gigi*, to bring me the same thing again. Owen choked on his vodka. "That's so... excessive," he said.

My neural pathways lead to multitude. Any appealing object sets off a desire for other objects similar in genus, design and function, related by colour, pattern, shape, provenance. The string of associations that said object unleashes comprises everything I've ever seen, touched, eaten, drunk, borrowed, lost, found, given, been given, bought, misplaced or read about. Anything can be Proust's madeleine: a linen towel, a cut-glass tumbler, a yellow rose, a pair of gloves, a duet in an opera, a tune playing on Spotify in a shop, a really good smoked trout mousse. Should that object be for sale, I'll spend money on assembling a family of associations. "No instant collections!" yelped a French boyfriend at the flea market as I became mesmerised by dour architectural prints of late 19th-century yellow brick factories. But the next booth had prints of sphinxes torn from a book about ancient Rome, and the associations they brought up – my grandmother's lamps, Oedipus, ancient Egypt, Jean Cocteau, winged women with animal lower halves – were richer than yellow brick factories. I still have some sphinxes.

I'm wired for plenty. A London shrink once jokingly diagnosed it as horror vacui; at the time, he was talking about my penchant for what is now called polyandry. But I see the world as divided into the excessives, who suffer from that fear of empty space – generous types with volatile tempers who believe More Is More – and the measured, who appreciate midcentury modern, purge their wardrobes and serve you one lamb chop at dinner. Horror vacui causes agoraphobia in Bauhaus rooms, can lead to body fat and, if unchecked, ends in hoarding. Freud certainly had it; the photographs of his study at Berggasse 19 show far too many little Egyptian and Greek statues lined up on his desk. No surprise that he's the father of free association.

I am surrounded by herds of contradictory associations, each one an elated response to a flea market or a journey to an interesting place, and these collections do not speak to one another. Five articulated brass fish; an ice bucket and various plated bar articles from the 1940s, and I don't even drink; God knows how many Hopi rattles – those gourds painted white, decorated with primary colours and adorned with feathers. The rattles, however, have no business on a shelf next to the remaining sphinxes. Did I mention that the floors are Kilim rug on petit point on Soumak on Ourika? There's no order to my excess.

Excess is more useful for the rich, whose money allows them to focus, or at least have enough room to allocate different spaces to their associations. In Palm Beach, Florida, I know a house that's a series of open pavilions set in a palm garden. In one, filigree shades edged in beads throw shards of light onto damask cushions on striped banquettes in front of tiles painted with turquoise curlicues and tulips. That room is the Topkapi harem room. Moroccan rugs and lamps and pots and baskets and many ewers and brass camels are gathered in the tented room across the garden, where dinner is served. That's order within excess.

Santoni

EDITED BY MARCO ZANINI

Modern Sex Work

Laura Watson and Sarah Walker both work for the English Collective of Prostitutes, the closest thing to a trade union that the approximately 70,000 female sex workers in the UK have. The ECP grew out of the feminist movement in the 1970s, although it counts "whorephobic" feminists among its most ardent critics. Recently, it has been making progress in its campaign to decriminalise prostitution. It now has the endorsement of Amnesty International, the passionate support of Hampshire Women's Institute and, it seems, the ear of Parliament's Home Affairs Select Committee.

Interview
Deborah Orr

Portrait
Katja Rahlwes

Deborah: Tell us how the ECP started.

Laura: There was a strike of French prostitutes in Lyon in 1975 – a murderer was on the loose and nothing was being done about it. Police corruption, mainly. So the prostitutes took refuge in a church in Lyon. There was a film made about it, which we showed here at the Crossroads Women's Centre in 2015, on the 40th anniversary of the strike. Women who were in a similar situation in England were inspired by their example.

Sarah: At that time it was impossible to be public about prostitution, so two young immigrant sex workers asked the feminist campaigner Selma James if she would be a spokeswoman for the organisation. From the beginning, the issues were decriminalising sex work, protection from violence, and getting other communities to support sex workers. In the 1970s, that was hard. A lot of women in the feminist movement dismissed sex workers as not part of the movement, and some even said that prostitutes were causing rape. It was awful. So it's been an uphill battle to where we are now, where there's much more understanding.

D: How did the two of you become involved?

S: There's been a long tradition of sex work in black communities – you know,

there's always somebody's auntie in sex work, or your sister-in-law. People have had to survive. There are stories that the anti-slavery movement was funded in part by sex workers sending money from places like San Francisco. When I was at university, it was obvious that prostitution was how a lot of students were making ends meet. Then the ECP held an occupation in Holy Cross Church in King's Cross, London, in 1982, and our women's group from university went. It just went from there.

L: I was brought up in a trade union family, and I've always felt very strongly about workers' rights and conditions and pay. I met the ECP and found it really encouraging that they focused on listening to sex workers to make legislation about sex work. We do casework, press, parliamentary work…

D: I've been aware of the ECP since the late 1990s, but the parliamentary symposium you ran in 2015, where you presented evidence in favour of decriminalisation, brought home to me that the ECP was a force to be reckoned with. Was that event a turning point?

L: Yes, it was packed, it was lively – it was really great. And the message of support from Amnesty International was a breakthrough; they are so respected.

They did a mapping exercise that found that criminalisation is having an absolutely horrendous impact on sex workers across the world. Women are being forced to work on their own, are being faced with violence. It also looked at the impact of poverty and the impact on immigrant and migrant women specifically – how a lack of options is pushing them into sex work.

D: Is that also the situation facing the women represented by the ECP?

L: In this country it's not illegal to exchange sex for money, but everything else women do – advertising, soliciting – is. The Police and Crime Act of 2009 increased the sentencing for brothel-keeping, which is when two or more sex workers are working together, and decreased the threshold on which the police can arrest you on the street. Essentially, they can now arrest you far more easily.

S: Hundreds of women who are just working together for safety come to the ECP for help. If one of you holds the keys to a flat or has the tenancy in your name, you could face a brothel-keeping conviction and seven years in prison. We were recently defending a woman facing three and a half years for brothel-keeping. She was a sex worker, not

Laura Watson
Sarah Walker

management, but the evidence against her was that when she opened the door to the police on several occasions, she was in her jeans and not her underwear.

L: The excuse the police often give for raiding — and they are raiding a lot now, without necessarily arresting or prosecuting people — is that they're looking for victims of trafficking. But what harassing those women does is drive them onto the streets, where it's more dangerous to work.

S: In London, sex workers are 12 times more likely to be murdered than other women. And in areas where there are high levels of criminalisation, women are far less likely to go to the police.

D: Is there evidence that violent men seek out sex workers because criminalisation makes prostitutes unlikely to report attacks?

L: There have been instances in cases we have fought where perpetrators have said, "We know you're not going to report this, so that's why we're targeting you." I think people are aware that it's less likely that anything will happen to them if they abuse a sex worker. The ECP, with Women Against Rape, did the first-ever private prosecution for rape, in 1995. Two sex workers were attacked by the same man and both of them, when they went to the police, were initially taken seriously, until they were found to be sex workers and then that was it. So the women took out a private prosecution, and the man was sent down for 14 years. He had attempted to kidnap another woman, and a whole violent history came out during the case.

S: When women come to us we try to get the police to put in writing that they will prioritise the violent attack over a prostitution offence. Criminalisation is one of the main things that prevent women from leaving sex work — nobody will hire you in another profession if you've got a sexual offence on your record, and it can be recorded as that rather than prostitution. Getting those off the books is what's needed — and we need to take all the laws off the book that criminalise almost everything that prostitutes do. They managed it in New Zealand; the Prostitution Reform Act of 2003 fully decriminalised sex work.

D: Removing criminal records for sex workers was among the recommendations made by the Home Affairs Select Committee in its interim report last July.

L: And we need them to stick to their recommendations, but also to go further, so we're still campaigning on those issues. In addition to the decriminalisation of sex workers on the street and indoors, we don't want clients criminalised, nor so-called "third parties": people like receptionists, bodyguards and the rest of it. But the committee hasn't even met since June's election.

S: In this country, we're always up against a lobby that wants to criminalise clients — kerb-crawling is already criminalised. And we know the impact of that crackdown. Sex workers still need to find clients — and going somewhere else means not being with their regular clientele in their local area, going to a place they don't know, getting into cars too quickly without time to negotiate or to check clients out. Recently, they have criminalised clients in the north of Ireland. That doesn't mean they're going to do it in the rest of the UK, but with it being party policy there and the DUP becoming part of the British government, we are very worried.

D: What would you say to those people — the DUP among them — whose first priority is to discourage sex work?

L: That moralistic view of prostitution leads to misinformation about who sex workers are, why they are working, what they think about the situation and the job, the wages, clients... They don't talk about why sex workers are going into prostitution.

S: Austerity is key. A 60 per cent increase in street prostitution in Doncaster was attributed to benefit sanctions. Most sex workers are working mothers.

D: You must have had high hopes for the election, with the shadow chancellor, John McDonnell, as your longstanding ally.

L: Yes, he's been our closest supporter. We've worked with him for many years.

S: I think one of the most important aspects of Labour's election campaign was that they said they want a society that's not punitive, and for that we need to end austerity. There's a group of women asylum seekers who meet at the centre, and they are destitute — they get £36 each a week. If you're in that situation, prostitution is one of the options to get yourself out of the poverty this government enforces. And that's what we want addressed. People talk about the discouragement of sex work, but they don't offer solutions to the driving forces behind women going into prostitution.

D: So does the ECP support women who wish to leave sex work?

L: Well, we don't encourage women to leave.

S: And for a lot of women, it's hard to match the wages you can make in sex work. It's not that you earn loads as a prostitute, but the hourly rate is generally higher than the minimum wage.

L: The overheads are definitely steeper if you're illegal. If, for example, your landlord finds out you're a sex worker, he might, typically, double the rent.

S: Women might need someone on the door, a maid, a security person. Then there's the cost of moving around when brothels are shut down after raids. And you don't necessarily want friends and family to know, and just the work of hiding that adds a whole set of extra expenses. All this instead of being able to report anything that goes wrong to the police without fear of arrest yourself, or, you know, accessing proper health services. Just taking part in society.

L: At the very least, there would be safety and an economy of scale if women were allowed to work together, indoors.

D: In an ideal world, would there be a place for prostitution?

S: For it to be an ideal world, a good many things would need to be rethought.

D: Roll on, roll on.

"In the UK it's not illegal to exchange sex for money, but everything else prostitutes do — advertising, soliciting — is."

NEHERA

Touring

A century of modernist ambition inspires this autumn's field trip as we step out with COS on the Glimpses of the Future architectural tours of London and Los Angeles for the enjoyment and edification of The Gentlewoman Club's members and readers alike.

COS x the gentlewoman

Photographed on location at the Isokon building in Hampstead, London.

The Touring Tote

The buildings of the modern period promised a healthier, happier future, and readers are invited to revisit that utopian dream using the enclosed map. Designed as a guide to the Glimpses of the Future expeditions staged by The Gentlewoman Club and COS earlier this September, the map provides extended routes around London's and LA's architectural gems to delight tourists and armchair travellers alike.

It fits perfectly into the inner pocket of this limited-edition tote bag, also produced for the tours. Made from padded Japanese nylon, it's the ideal travel companion and is available from COS stores in both cities. Photography by Chris Rhodes, styling by Eliza Conlon.

thegentlewoman.com/club
cosstores.com

WOOLRICH SINCE 1830
AMERICA'S OLDEST OUTDOOR CLOTHING COMPANY

WOOLRICH
JOHN RICH & BROS.

woolrich.eu

Underarm hair

There are beauty trends that unite generations. Is there anything more glorious than a braided silver fringe? But there's one subject that acts like a fault line – the length of one's underarm hair. Should the sight of an undepilated armpit throw a woman into a Pavlovian panic, conjuring flashbacks to second-wave debates on personal politics and body shame, the likelihood is she's a Gen Xer or older. Because according to the market researchers Mintel, her little sisters have fewer hang-ups when it comes to their axillary areas. Over the past three years, the number of UK women under the age of 25 denuding their underarms has dropped by 18 per cent.

Whether it's a style thing, a pheromonal thing or an unexpected gift from our more gender-fluid age remains a mystery. Maybe they just like the way it looks.

Photography by Chloé Le Drezen. Model: Lucie Rox.

By Gert Jonkers

I've been drunk, I've smoked grass and I've always enjoyed that bit where they sing in yoga classes, but until recently I'd never had a gong bath. I surely made up for this at the Big Pause, a retreat in the cork-tree wilderness of southern Spain. There, I didn't just have one gong bath but five. In a week. Five!

Gong bath number one occurred on arrival. I had no idea what to expect and, just to be sure, wore my bathing trunks under my tracksuit. Who knew a gong bath didn't involve an actual bath? We, a group of eight participants, lay on the roof terrace under wool blankets as the time passed beneath a magnificent sky full of stars. We closed our eyes. We did some meditative breathing. Someone blew a conch, its call echoing for miles over the surrounding rolling hills. I mean, I could have died peacefully then and there.

Then it started.

From the shiny bronze Paiste gong that I recognised from news footage of a big company celebrating its IPO at the stock exchange, I expected some sort of massive, meditative *bong... bong... bong... bong*. Not in a million years could I have anticipated what unfolded. What was this? Was it sound? Was it a feeling? Was it abstract? I heard whispers, roars, a symphonic orchestra. I dozed off. I slept and dreamed and thought somebody was playing "Stanlow", my favourite track from Orchestral Manoeuvres in the Dark's second album, and the middle part of New Order's "Blue Monday", where it sounds like a jet fighter roars over just before they sing "I see a ship in the harbour." I dreamed of green meadows and a dark blue tunnel. When the sound finally subsided, I felt both drowsy and rejuvenated. This magical interlude had happened over about 45 minutes, but it could have been a day, or a whole lifetime for that matter.

In the following days I had four more gong baths, eliciting more hallucinations of things exciting and forbidden. At one point I honestly thought I was levitating. Later, I learned that what I was experiencing was a physical phenomenon called entrainment, the power of vibrations to align less powerful vibrations. It's an effect that can apparently be proven by putting several pendulum clocks together in one room: leave them going for a day and they'll end up ticking perfectly in sync. The gong's rich overtones were aligning my subtle brainwaves. So while a normal thinking mind may be buzzing at somewhere between 14 and 40 hertz, the gong forced my brain to lower the hertzes it was emitting, all the way down to relaxation (8 to 13 hertz), REM sleep (5 to 7 hertz) and even deep, dreamless sleep (0.5 to 4 hertz). Ever had that jet-lag feeling of being pushed into a nap, as if you're dipping into another state of consciousness for a few floaty minutes with no way to resist? That's how this felt. The gong managed what I've always been promised meditation would achieve: to take me to that "other" state. And instead of me having to do it all by myself, this sonic gong power gently forced my brain to slow down.

I'm sure the mystical environment of the retreat made the gong feel even more magical. But if entrainment is scientifically proven, why wouldn't it work in the metropolitan panic of Islington, Belleville or Amsterdam West, where one can easily enrol in a gong session? I'm just a bit luckier: from now on, the sound of the gong won't only take me to a calmer state but also, somehow, back to Spain.

7016 Feng pewter bronze gong. Photography by Chloé Le Drezen.

Entrainment.

Leather Beach

Pleated, whip-stitched or bejazzled with rocks, the definitive outfits come in one material this season, and one colour: black. Photography by Andrea Spotorno, styling by Alex Harrington.

Leather Beach

Above, water-repellent leather trousers with zip detail by HERMÈS and faux-leather Vienna polo-neck top by JOSEPH. The calfskin zipper boots (worn throughout) are by ALAÏA.

On the opening page, a lamb's-leather coat by ALAÏA over a pleated nappa-leather skirt by DION LEE.

An asymmetrical pleated leather skirt with white detail and arched hemline by PROENZA SCHOULER under a polyester-mix shift dress by PHILOSOPHY DI LORENZO SERAFINI.

A leather off-the-shoulder asymmetrical minidress is embellished with SWAROVSKI crystal embroidery. It's by SAINT LAURENT by Anthony Vaccarello.

The midi skirt by SPORTMAX comes in vinyl; here, it's worn under a tank-top dress by LOEWE that's in viscose. But the black boots with zippers by ALAÏA? They're leather.

Leather Beach

A lamb's-leather wrap skirt with red lining by BY MALENE BIRGER
under a sleeveless jacket with leather pockets and white topstitching
by LOUIS VUITTON.

Soft leather just kisses the shoulder in the minidress from Anthony Vacarello's thigh-skimming autumn collection for SAINT LAURENT. Skin on skin, you might say.

A lamb's-leather shift dress with crimson, fuchsia and white leather whip-stitching by ALEXANDER McQUEEN over a calfskin asymmetrical skirt by JIL SANDER.

Leather Beach

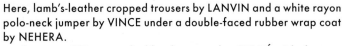

Here, lamb's-leather cropped trousers by LANVIN and a white rayon polo-neck jumper by VINCE under a double-faced rubber wrap coat by NEHERA.

On page 133, a cracked-leather coat by CHLOÉ with dog-ear collar over the white polo-neck jumper by VINCE.

Above, a calfskin and lamb's-leather patchwork dress by CÉLINE.

Model: Charlee Fraser at IMG. Hair: Ramona Eschbach at Total Management. Make-up: Anthony Preel at Artlist. Casting: Adam Hindle at Streeters. Photographic assistance: Pete Hawk. Styling assistance: Luca Galasso, Megan Soria. Production: Bird Production.

Julie de Libran

Modern Left Bank

Julie de Libran's immaculately manicured hands belie the fact that the artistic director of Sonia Rykiel spent her teenage years bussing dishes at her father's California restaurant. The experience taught her that tips weren't the only perks of working hard. Twenty-five years later, having learned the secrets of the fashion industry at the sides of designers such as Ferré, Prada and, latterly, Marc Jacobs at Louis Vuitton, Julie, 45, is reaping the benefits of this early life lesson. In the three years she's been at the helm of the quintessentially Parisian house of Rykiel, she's made coquettish cool again, thanks in part to her strong work ethic.

Interview
Andrew Tucker

Portraits
Katja Rahlwes

Julie: So, ask me whatever you like. Just not what brand of conditioner I use.

Andrew: My guess would be Kérastase.

J: I've been told in the past that's the kind of thing readers want, but I'd rather talk about my work. Still, maybe I'll share some secrets with you — if you're lucky.

A: People now know you for Rykiel, but you seem to have been everywhere — Ferré, Versace, Prada and Vuitton. What drives you so hard?

J: Well, I've had a job since I was 12 years old. I grew up in California, and it was quite normal to start babysitting when you were young. By 14, I was helping to manage my father's restaurant.

A: What, at 14? That's slave labour!

J: No, it was good for me. I'd go there after school on my Vespa. I'd serve the food, manage the team — it was a French bistro. Of course, I really wanted to work in a fashion boutique, but my dad wouldn't let me.

A: The typical boss's daughter?

J: No, no, no. I was quite a timid teenager. I was always the girl who'd shrink into her seat when the teacher asked someone to speak. Working in the restaurant forced me to interact — to speak to adults, take orders, give orders. It toughened me up.

A: And you got paid.

J: Pocket money, really, which I'd spend on clothes. But it made me independent — that was the most important thing.

A: Clearly. At 18 you went to study in Milan. Quite a culture shock.

J: Oh yes. Even though I grew up in Aix-en-Provence and I spent my teenage summers there with cousins, Italy was still a shock to the system. The weather wasn't exactly like San Diego, and the people were so different. It was 1990, and every other woman seemed to be wearing a pleated skirt, like a uniform. It was so smart and formal, and I was still a Cali girl at heart — sun-bleached hair, gold hoop earrings, white T-shirts and faded Levi's. But the move taught me another important lesson: how to adapt.

A: Where did you study?

J: At the Istituto Marangoni. I did a shorter course as an overseas student — a year and a half. And immediately afterwards I landed a job with Ferré, when he was at Dior but with an HQ in Milan.

A: Wow, Gianfranco Ferré — that's a blast from the past! He had a fearsome reputation.

J: He was a terrifying man. I've never encountered anyone since who would scream so much — tantrums that went on for days over something as insignificant as dropping a hem three centimetres. It bordered on the ridiculous. He was as big as an opera singer, but he could run up and down stairs like a teenager. And he was incredibly talented and worked like a maniac. I learned so much from being there.

A: What, exactly?

J: Ferré taught me discipline. He taught me how the fashion world functioned. I'd barely turned 20, and I was working on these huge productions. It really was another era. I remember doing fittings on Kate Moss while Carla Bruni was singing and playing her guitar where she waited. And the fittings themselves were insane. We would have these closets full of toiles — trousers in different

Julie de Libran

silhouettes, his trademark white organza shirts with embellished cuffs and jewelled cufflinks. I'd help Ferré fit them on the model and help with the fabric selection, and he would sketch furiously all the while. Then I'd take the drawings to the workroom, where we'd have to decipher them. Those were the days when everything was made from scratch — fabrics, embroideries, jewellery. It was a proper old-fashioned atelier.

A: Difficult?

J: He was a little kinder to me because I was still so young, but you had to watch your step. I didn't really have a life; it was just hard, hard work. But it was my choice. Plus, I've never been one to party, not then and not now. Then, as you hit your 30s, your priorities change again, especially when you have kids. You make choices, and you end up knowing yourself better as a result. I appreciate I'm lucky I can pursue my passion. I couldn't be a stay-at-home mum.

A: Did your mum work?

J: Yes, and she still does. One of my earliest memories on arriving in California when I was eight was seeing my mum — her name is Corine de Libran Longanbach — start working as an interior designer. It was 1980 when she began importing French antiques all the way to Rancho Santa Fe, long before anyone else even thought of it. Now she's working on three houses for a client in Japan. I'm really proud of her.

A: That work ethic again. So are you a nice boss?

J: Well, I expect hard work; this isn't an industry where you count the hours until you've got the job done. It should be a bit of a vocation for everyone, but I'm mindful that we all have lives outside the business. And I respect my team — my main two assistants are English and Italian, but the team are also French, Chinese and Japanese. I like the different viewpoints they bring. For example, being eccentric wasn't encouraged in my own fashion education, so I relish that English approach — that knowledge of fashion history that is deliberately subverted. But I also admire the understatement of the Italians and the studied inelegance of the French.

A: Is your team relatively stable, or have you ever had to fire anyone?

J: A few — it's an inevitable part of the job. I had to do a really hard one when I was at Louis Vuitton, and it just felt terrible. But you have to learn to separate the personal and professional.

A: Actually a tough boss!

J: I prefer the French term *exigeante*. Although the American in me would say "Business is business."

A: So what does a demanding boss's day look like?

J: Well, we begin work at 10 — it's the French way. I get up at 7.30 because I need to be a mum, and I try to fit in some exercise. I cycle to the office, so no boring commute! Then I often finish about 9.30pm because there's so much to do — atelier fittings, shoe fittings, bags, knitwear, communication, ad campaign meetings. It's a vast number of roles.

A: But you love it?

J: It's wonderful. I know there's debate about whether today's designers are more like brand managers than pure creatives, but I don't see why we can't be both. Plus, this is what my career has built me up to do. At Prada, it was my role to work with celebrities, which at the time was an entirely new venture for the brand. At Vuitton, my role was multifaceted, from presenting the collections to working on the set design for the shows. I like that variety. Sonia Rykiel may be a well-known brand, but it's not a huge business, which means I can integrate everything I need to do without going insane. And I'm privileged to be able to create beautiful things for a living.

A: We've hardly touched on the clothes. Tell me about a beautiful thing that makes you happy.

J: Pockets! Keeping my hands in my pockets makes me feel secure. Whether they're practical or not, I insist that we add them to every garment at Rykiel — even in a sheer mousseline dress. We call those "theatre pockets"; they're simple slits in the fabric that don't necessarily have a pocket bag but give you somewhere to put your hands.

A: A place for everything and everything in its place. It sounds as if your work offers you everything you need.

J: To be honest, I'm curious about many other things — but they might have to wait until I'm older. I'd like to improve my photography skills, paint a bit more, and I'd love to improve my writing.

A: You write?

J: I've always written for therapy. I've kept diaries since I was about 10.

A: And are they for your eyes only?

J: Put it this way: if my husband read them it would be at his own risk. I used to keep them hidden, but what with moving around so much, they're mostly stacked on shelves in plain sight. I did once have a very jealous Italian boyfriend who read them and got really pissed off, but mostly no one's been brave enough to try.

A: Do you write every day?

J: Yes. I write at night and fill one or two pages, depending on what I have to say. I use a black fineliner — never blue — and an Hermès agenda.

A: Pricey!

J: Well, they do accumulate. For a long time I never missed a day. Now I'm not so obsessive, but if I'm away from it for too long I have to go back and recuperate. It's the way I externalise my inner life.

A: Would you ever look in someone else's diary if they left it out?

J: I don't know. I'd try my best not to. As a kid I would sneak into my mum's wardrobe and open all my Christmas presents and then rewrap them — so perhaps I would. Who knows?

A: That's all documented in the teenage volumes, is it?

J: They're mainly clichéd boyfriend dramas. It's funny — there's a standing joke among my friends that if you've forgotten what happened on a certain day, just ring Julie and she'll be able to tell you.

Fourteen-year-old Julie was in esteemed company on her scooter; other notable Vespa enthusiasts have included John Wayne, Charlton Heston, Jayne Mansfield and Marlon Brando.

"Am I a tough boss? I prefer the French term *exigeante.* Although the American in me would say business is business."

MY SISTER LEONETTA PORTRAYED BY OUR MOTHER MARIA SILVIA

London
109, Mount street

Rome
Via Del Governo Vecchio, 67

delfinadelettrez.com

By Marina O'Loughlin

In my tiny, rarefied world – that of newspaper restaurant critics – arguments on the subject of anonymity have raged ever since the role was formalised sometime during the 1950s. Whether or not anonymity is important or even necessary is hotly debated. I'm one of a dwindling anonymous bunch – there are no public photos; the photographic byline on my weekly *Guardian* newspaper column features me (well, not actually me) with my face covered by a large dinner plate. Visually, no record of me exists.

I don't remember the exact moment I decided that anonymity was going to be my lot. But I do remember the reasoning. On the one hand, it was all loftiness and integrity – you can't report objectively on any institution that you're in bed with, be it food or art or politics. I believed that then and I believe it now. A restaurant might not be able to change intrinsically once a critic is recognised, but the experience most certainly will.

And on the other hand, I'm just not very sociable. Years ago, when psychographic tests were all the rage in the kind of primary-coloured ad agencies in which I used to work, my Myers-Briggs test results put me in solitary, in my own "silo". (About which my boss memorably asked the entire office, "Do we really need that silo?") And when I moved to London from a much smaller city, I loved the fact that nobody knew or cared who I was. I could behave how I liked – unsuitable liaisons, unfortunate wardrobe choices, unwise bouts of drunken country-and-western singing – without whispers or recriminations. I don't like parties, though in the early days I was naively thrilled to be invited to high-profile food-scene events. It didn't take me long to realise that when you have to pretend to be your friend's cousin from Up North, they're the dullest occasions imaginable. Suddenly, nobody's interested in talking to you. No, I enjoy being the cat who walks alone (with a plus one over the dinner table).

In this social media-infected age, where everyone is party to everyone else's absolutely everything, anonymity seems wilful, contrary. And it's downright tricky. How do you pay when a credit card bears your name, for example? What I thought was a wizard wheeze – paying with a card in my married name – crashed and burned when I idiotically agreed to a throwaway newspaper piece about what the spouses of food people do for Valentine's Day. So now I find myself taking wads of cash around with me like a second-hand car dealer. And because websites demand an email address, I'm one of the few people who uses the telephone in this age of online booking – withholding my number so restaurants don't have a record of it. I do have a couple of online aliases, but I can never remember the passwords for them, or which one I've used. It's taken me a while, but I've finally learned to put my chosen alias beside each booking on my calendar. It seems simple in retrospect, but it took a lot of trial and error to get here.

All the subterfuge can venture into the bizarre, though. At one point, I started using my husband's phone number for bookings, but the savvier restaurants got wind of this and he was bemused to find himself whisked to the front of queues and given unbidden drinks when at business meetings over lunch. Many of the bigger establishments have cheat sheets – headshots of the major critics for spotting purposes – which I've occasionally caught sight of. I'm a silhouette. Which is fine. What's galling are the accompanying bios: one of my colleagues was described as "tall and glamorous"; mine simply reads "tweets a lot."

There have been occasions when I've realised, with an encroaching prickly feeling, that I've been clocked. It mostly happens when a particularly beady publicist has managed to infer information about me from social media burblings: my accent, my friendship group, my predilection for a frosty martini. This results in what the – formerly anonymous – *New York* magazine critic Adam Platt described as "the strange, time-honoured Kabuki dance that takes place

Anonymity.

between chefs and restaurateurs and the people whose job it is to cover them." They pretend they don't know who you are to pay lip service to the deception; you pretend you haven't noticed that they've noticed... Oh, it's a whole lot of fun for all the family.

But there's a more toxic subtext to anonymity these days: that of trolling and fake news. It is widely held that, psychologically, anonymity lessens the feeling of accountability. As someone who publishes but is also very active online, in a weird marriage of visibility and invisibility, I think my anonymity protects me from the anonymous. I believe I suffer less online abuse than some of my female peers simply because the trolls can't box me under "fuckable" or "unfuckable". In fact, there has been speculation that I'm a man, or a hive mind of several people – which is not, I feel, entirely flattering to my writing.

By choosing anonymity, you also choose a degree of penury. It is undeniably tough to earn a decent living as an anonymous creative. Author or artist, fashion designer or performer, the loot usually pours in via personal appearances, whether in the flesh or – oh lucrative joy – a television profile. There are, of course, exceptions: the singer Sia managed quite a few years before she unmasked. And Elena Ferrante's anonymity – more correctly pseudonymity – didn't curtail her bestselling career. She has eloquently outlined the reason for her decision: not wishing her work to be involved in the "circus of personality" of "the celebrity author", wanting it to be judged and read solely on its own terms. And when she was outed it was met with anger, outrage and accusations of sexism from the literary world.

I can see both sides, up to a point. And here's where I have to confess to regularly wearing another hat: I'm also a travel writer for *BBC Good Food* magazine, a job that is impossible to do while anonymous. I have to meet people – for tours, for background information, for insight into the local scene impossible to glean from any amount of distant research. And when I pack my suitcase to leave the country, I leave my cloak of anonymity behind.

It's remarkable to witness the difference between visiting somewhere as a known entity and slinking in unannounced: suddenly, the best tables are at my disposal, extra dishes mysteriously arrive from the kitchen, a glass of champagne and delicious dessert wines will bookend my meal. I don't care what my "out" colleagues protest – it's a lot harder to remain dispassionate when you've been showered with love. And then the worst bit: the chef, a look of pained anxiety on his or her face, will issue from behind the scenes to ask how everything was. In the pantheon of awkward social interactions, this one ranks close to the top. I find myself turning into the little old ladies from *Fawlty Towers*. "Lovely! It was all lovely!"

Although there's something seductive about anonymity in these share-all times, gently, ever so gently, I'm making myself a tiny bit more visible. The irony that a lot of it is due to social media is not lost on me – Twitter, in particular, is an invaluable resource for insider recommendations when travelling and, if you're travelling alone, it's good to be able to meet those like-minded, helpful people for a drink. I even spoke on radio for the first time recently, something I'd always avoided out of fear that my accent might be a dead giveaway – as if I'm the only Scottish person ever to visit a restaurant. But if I were to give up anonymity completely, I'm not sure the benefits would outweigh the downsides. Even in seen-it-all London, I've eaten with famous critics and felt the atmosphere petrify as soon as they walked through the door. So, come out once and for all? I've learned to never say never, but I suspect I'll lurk in the shadows just a little bit longer.

Jewelry as poetry.

CATBIRDNYC.COM

Mount Wilson

Reaching the summit is a thrill, but the descent may take a different course. Setting off in workwear should help to keep impromptu rambles on the right path. Photography by Clara Balzary, styling by Jason Rider.

Mount Wilson

The model Ansley Gulielmi was born in Chicago but loves nothing more than escaping to an Alaskan cabin with a good book. Here in California's San Gabriel Mountains, she wears an oatmeal-coloured cotton jersey jacket by COS over a white merino wool Catkin polo-neck by JOHN SMEDLEY with black nylon Camp shorts by BATTEN-WEAR. The black Big Bop bag is from MYSTERY RANCH.

On the previous page, a black corduroy work shirt jacket by MHL, a grey cotton turtleneck by L.L. BEAN and white cotton drill Painter's Pants by DICKIES are ideal for tackling the downward trip. The grey cotton socks are by FALKE, the white Eric 8368 trainers are by RUCO LINE and the moss green Anly shopper is by NORSE PROJECTS.

The climb down Mount Wilson continues, in a vintage red nylon anorak by THE NORTH FACE over a white cotton polo-neck jumper with ruffle detail and blue denim Broome Street jeans, both by KATE SPADE NEW YORK. The grey socks are by FALKE and the white putty-leather Army trainers are by MHL.

Mount Wilson

Mobile telephone signals are unreliable on Mount Wilson, so alternative amusements must be found. Oversized denim jacket with seam detail and washed loose denim jeans both by TOPSHOP; lime green ribbed silk-and-wool polo-neck by BEAUTIFUL PEOPLE; grey FALKE socks; black suede Sneaker loafers with tassel bow detail by FITFLOP.

Ansley takes in the view wearing a vintage navy-and-charcoal cotton zip-front sweatshirt over a navy-and-white cotton turtleneck by L.L. BEAN and grey wool wide-legged tailored trousers by COS. Grey socks by FALKE; white leather trainers by MHL, as before. The Sure Shot AF35M film camera is from CANON.

Mount Wilson

Seventeen-year-old Ansley is more of a runner than a walker and advises a hearty intake of vegetables and water for long distances. She strides on in a vintage blue corduroy jacket by LEVI'S, navy pin-striped wool-and-cotton trousers by TOAST, beige cotton socks by FALKE and grey felted wool Amsterdam clogs by BIRKENSTOCK.

She makes a pit stop, wearing black cotton canvas Turner bib over-alls by CARHARTT WIP over a black-and-white striped silk-and-cotton Minimal shirt by MARGARET HOWELL. The grey wool turtleneck is vintage, the beige cotton socks are by FALKE and the clogs are by BIRKENSTOCK. The Eddy water bottle is from CAMELBAK.

Mount Wilson

Ansley reaches the foothills and makes a break for it. She wears a cotton flannel tartan shirt by DSQUARED2 over a navy-and-green striped Railroad polo-neck by VINCE and navy Camp shorts by BATTENWEAR. The grey socks are by FALKE and the black Courchevel leather and navy suede Rowan penny loafers are by JOHN LOBB.

Binoculars, 10 x 42 magnification, from CALIFORNIA SURPLUS MART.
Model: Ansley Gulielmi at Ford Models. Hair: Nikki Providence at Forward Artists. Make-up: Sandy Ganzer at Forward Artists. Casting: Noah Shelley at AM Casting. Photographic assistance: Tim Mahoney. Styling assistance: Megan King. Production: Rosco Production.

BE FELT

vince.com

vince.

Helen McCrory

Modern Stages

Helen McCrory will gladly sign autographs for fans who loved her as Narcissa Malfoy from *Harry Potter* or Aunt Polly from *Peaky Blinders*. But the Paddington-born actress is just as likely to be found treading the boards of the National. Inspired by seeing Judi Dench on stage in *Mother Courage* as a schoolgirl, Helen has spent 27 years building a reputation as one of British drama's most fearless stars. Now 49 and the recipient of an OBE in this year's honours list, the roles are hers for the taking. That is, so long as she can coordinate schedules with her husband, Damian Lewis, who's also pretty busy.

Interview
Penny Martin

Portraits
Katja Rahlwes

←
Helen is wearing a white striped cotton shirt by SUNSPEL with her own jeans, socks, trainers and hat. On page 155, she adds a double-breasted navy wool trench coat by PAUL SMITH and a brushed yellow mohair hooded cardigan by CHLOÉ.

Penny: I spent several hours yesterday in the National Theatre's archive, watching a video of you in Terence Rattigan's *The Deep Blue Sea*. Even so, I had no idea how petite you are.

Helen: Oh, God, that's very diligent of you!

P: The Lyttleton is such a vast stage to fill, standing up there on your own. But then you've such a big, resonant voice.

H: My dad always used to say, with his typical Glaswegian charm, "You've lungs that could shatter glass!" But you know, you don't go to see a play, you go to *hear* a play. That's what people used to say.

P: Is that so?

H: Yes. You don't run a bath, you *draw* a bath. Likewise, you hear a play. And I think you do have to hear it. It's inexcusable when you go to the theatre and can't hear someone speak. An actor is their character's advocate; your job is to understand all their complexities and portray them as clearly and as truthfully as possible. There's no point in fucking mumbling at the back!

P: You're also brilliant at accents. Is that something you have to work on?

H: Definitely. I think acting is a craft, not an art. You should work on every part of your body. Different roles require different things. When I was playing Medea, I would eat blood-red steaks with fried eggs on top to keep my energy levels up. I gather they've done research about what actors are putting their bodies through by going on stage, and adrenaline-wise, it's the equivalent of a car crash. At the end of *The Deep Blue Sea*'s run, I think I was a stone lighter, and I eat a lot — much more than Damian. And you should always be working on your voice so that your character has different tones as well as accents. I actually just came down from Birmingham this morning, where I'd been filming *Peaky* and doing a voiceover — I'm the new voice of Marks & Spencer.

P: Are you really? Do you get to say "This isn't just *any* chocolate pudding — it's a Belgian ganache soufflé pudding"?

H: Oh, no, it's all "Spend it well" now. I went into that session directly from doing Polly in *Peaky Blinders*, who speaks right down here. I listened to recordings of the women from the Small Heath and Garrison Lane districts of Birmingham, where *Peaky* is filmed, in the oral history archive of Birmingham library, and they smoked a *lot*. Polly sounds like she's just had a nice sleep. So I automatically started off down there, with "M&S...", you know, and the client was like, "Woah!" and I was straight back up to that tighter clippedness.

P: Is that your natural pitch? The real McCrory?

H: It's a version of me. I've always been more interested in transforming into someone else than playing myself. Some actors' strength is in playing themselves; you go to see them to witness their charisma.

Helen McCrory

P: Who's a good example of that?

H: Clint Eastwood. You don't want him to rock up in drag; you want to see Clint Eastwood. And then there are other actors, and I count myself among them, who most enjoy not being recognisable. And I like to make it really authentic where I can. When I played Jo in *Streetlife* with Rhys Ifans — one of my first film roles, playing a girl from the estate — I went to the estate to get my hair bleached. The hair and make-up team said, "Your hair is falling out; you've got bald patches." And I was like, "Yes, that's what happens when you get it done for £3.50."

P: It sounds time-consuming, all that research.

H: That's the thing. If you're working on *The Deep Blue Sea* at the National, Carrie Cracknell, the director, will bring all that in. We'll have psychologists come to talk to us about the suicide attempt right at the beginning of the play, and we'll have historians talk to us about how serving in the war affected people, since there's a pilot in the cast of characters. Everybody's in the room, and everybody hears it. And this is so bizarre to me. You're paid £2.50 a week doing a play, and yet there are all those resources. Then film and TV is far more lucrative — it's subsidising your theatre work, basically — but you're doing all the research yourself. I spend far more time on that than I do on my lines. You can always tell which parts Damian and I are being offered at any given moment from the books and diaries scattered around our bed. Everything from Thomas Aquinas to Kenneth Tynan to Hemingway to a tome on 18th-century tattoos.

P: Are you considering getting inked?

H: That was for *Penny Dreadful*. There's a moment at the beginning of the second season where I'm in a bath of blood, smoking a cigarette, singing a song. And I step out, completely nude, and my whole body is covered in tattoos.

P: I was interested to read that you decided to take on more sexually driven roles on returning to acting after having your children.

H: I think I had played those parts before — I played Anna Karenina, and obviously she's very driven sexually by Vronsky, and I played Barbara Villiers, Charles II's mistress. But the difference was that I hadn't shown anything.

P: Of your body?

H: Yes. When Joe Wright gave me *Charles II* in 2003, I think there were 32 counts of nudity. I said, "That's absolutely beautiful. I'll do the nude scenes. But you won't show my body."

P: That must have taken some doing. In the second season of *Peaky Blinders*, where Aunt Polly is subjected to a brutal sexual assault, I felt like I'd seen a great deal of your body, but in fact perhaps all I actually saw was a lot of your back.

H: Yes, exactly — you get it. I don't have a problem with being naked; what I have a problem with is the control over how I am depicted. I think it's to do with growing up in Africa — my father was a diplomat, and in east Africa people are very modest. They don't walk around with everything hanging out. So I was never that person, really. I've had a few directors ask me to do more explicit scenes, and I'd go, "Oh, no, thanks." It never upset me, and it never seemed to upset them very much either.

P: Your success came so early, playing Rose Trelawny in Richard Eyre's production of *Trelawny of the "Wells"* at the National just out of drama school. It might have been easy to be exploited. I've read you credit the Drama Centre as giving you a really good grounding.

H: Yes, because they were really honest. I remember my parents saying to me, "Lots of people can act. Whether they are happy and satisfied by an actor's life is a different matter. Can you cope with constant rejection? Are you a personality that thrives on that?" So when I auditioned for the Centre and they said, "Why are you doing *Romeo and Juliet*? Have you ever been in love?" and I went, "I haven't," they said, "Well, why do you think people of 50 or 60 are going to sit in the audience and listen to you talk about love?" And I thought, They're bloody right! And that's why I wanted to go there — that idea that you're not born an actress: you become one.

P: So now you're 49, are you qualified to talk about love? You've been married for, what, 10 years?

H: Yes, exactly, and it's completely surprised me. I had no idea how different it would make you feel in the world, being part of a gang. Damian and I just don't stop talking. I had 10 minutes between arriving in London today and getting here, so we just took a walk to the end of our street, talking about all the gardens, what we've got to do, when are we going to Reykjavik? Then, he was offered this job, and I remembered I've been offered that job for next year! "Have you read it? No? OK, let's read it during half-term..."

P: You come across particularly well together in public. How do you feel about being seen as a power couple?

H: Well, if it's a film screening or something, when you walk down the red carpet and somebody says, "Hello, this is the BBC," I don't think you can go, "Oh, I hate doing interviews, I hate dressing up." You'd think, "You ungrateful bitch!" I do feel lucky. But the awful thing about marriage is that no one else is as interesting afterwards, are they? If I'm at a party, it's not quite as good when he's not there. I'm not saying we spend our days skipping through buttercups, holding hands, but I'm pretty happy.

P: Maybe you should write a wellness guide for other actors.

H: Ha. No, I have such respect for writing, but I prefer interpreting. As a storyteller, you are in total control of your own narrative. If you choose your words well, it doesn't matter how it ends — if you decide it's a happy ending, it's a happy ending.

The same ominous phrase appears at least once in every episode of HBO's gothic hit television series *Penny Dreadful*: "And then?"

"I don't have a problem with being naked; what I have a problem with is how I am depicted."

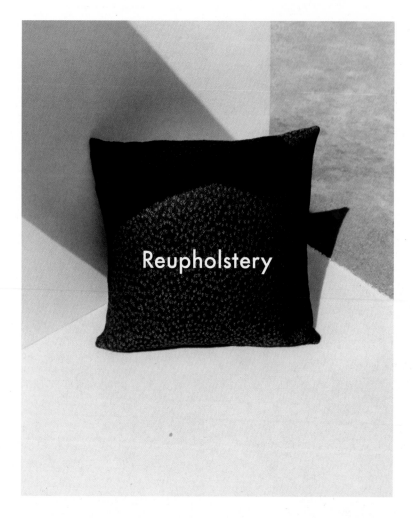

Reupholstery

When you finally get round to re-covering that threadbare damask chaise longue, the upholsterer will advise you to select a sturdy neutral cloth. Getting the thing out of the house and finding an affordable workshop will prove such a trauma that you might be tempted to forgo fashionable colour and pattern because this is a once-in-a-lifetime affair. Even Raf Simons, designer of the luscious Kvadrat material covering this cushion, agrees that such projects can be daunting. "There's furniture in my house that's needed to be reupholstered for years," he says. But once Raf finally goes for it, he'll select a fabric every bit as precious and personal as one he would wear – maybe something like the Ria, pictured. "It's curious it's taken me so long; I'm a very decisive person. I don't have this problem choosing a Prada coat."

Ria no 791 upholstery fabric by KVADRAT by Raf Simons. Photography by Chloé Le Drezen.

CLOSED

CLOSED.COM
#CLOSEDOFFICIAL

FAIR. SINCE 1978.

GOLD—
SMITHS'
FAIR

Precious Mysteries
26 September – 8 October 2017
Closed 2 October

Fine Jewellery and Contemporary Silver
goldsmithsfair.co.uk
#goldsmithsfair

Lost-property umbrella

The seasoned diner might feel confident asking to be seated further from the ember barbecue or for a black napkin instead of a white. But who'd be so bold as to stride up to the cloakroom at the end of a meal and demand an umbrella from the lost-property box? Claire Ptak, that's who. A pastry chef at Chez Panisse in the 1990s and now proprietor of Violet bakery in Hackney, east London, she's cooked her way around the world, picking up "abandoned" umbrellas wherever she eats. The police in England and Wales haven't taken lost-property reports since 2014, she insists; it's not so much a legal question, then, more one of restaurant policy versus front. So make like Claire and ask for your heart's desire – a 1960s clear style, perhaps, that'll double up as a parasol.

Japanese clear folding umbrella from TOKYO LAB. Photography by Chloé Le Drezen.

By Kate Finnigan

There are notions we pin to ourselves like little flags. Not so big as to be considered beliefs, rather preferences or predilections that become pass notes to who we are. We should hand them out to strangers; it would save time.

I don't wear pink lipstick. I only ever wear black eyeliner. I no longer read books by American males. I am a one-on-one person. My scenery preference is woods and hills rather than sea and sand. I'm a trousers woman. I don't wear earrings.

I did not wear earrings. Not as a child, not as a teenager, not in my 20s, not when I was married, not when I became a mother. It was one of my things. I'm tempted to put it down to Catholicism, the purity of the virgin lobe, et cetera. But then I always got swoony over the Elizabethan pierced ear – Shakespeare's single hoop in the Chandos portrait was hot.

There is great comfort to be had in our certainties. But one of the joys of getting older, I've found, is in letting go. Releasing those little flags into the zenith. Enjoying the relief of surrender. For 40 years I didn't wear earrings, and when I was 41 I changed my mind.

I had already started to see the benefits in having little stars of light about the face, and to appreciate the earring's potential to change the mood of an outfit – from serious to casual, from dressed-down to unexpectedly expensive around the cheekbones. And when I met a striking Italian woman in Milan wearing one of Delfina Delettrez's single vivid blue evil-eye earrings, I felt a metaphysical pull that took me right back to Shakespeare's sexy hoop.

You can surrender by degrees. Perhaps start by ordering some pale yellow citrine stones wrapped in fine gold chain several months before you have your ears pierced. You may not be able to wear them, but, like buying condoms before a date, their possession contains an illicit thrill of anticipation. And then, three months later, you attend a party with Kevin the Piercer and within 15 minutes find yourself with a trio of (relatively painless) new chinks in your lobes – two in the right, one in the left – inhabited by tiny white pearl studs.

It was a rush. Better than a new lipstick, better than going blond. They made me feel both more girlish and more womanly. Yes, it stung a bit and the wait for healing was irritating, but it was an excellent talking point and met with general approval. (The one exception was my six-year-old daughter, who was horrified by the punctures and wept repeatedly about "never being able to kiss my ears again".)

I don't wear earrings all the time – and not only because I keep losing them. But when I look in the mirror and they're not in, I see myself as incomplete, unfinished. Yet how daft it is to feel defined by wearing jewellery. As daft as not reading novels by American men. The hard lines I once drew for myself are more blurred now, rubbed out entirely in parts. I am 43 and inconsistent. All my life I didn't wear earrings, and now I sometimes do.

Serti sur Vide pink-gold and five-emerald-cut-diamond earring by REPOSSI. Photography by Chloé Le Drezen. Model: Julia Wieliczko at Viva Model Management. Manicure: Mike Pocock at Saint Luke Artist Management. Set design: Staci-Lee Hindley.

Surrender.

DROMe

Booted

Autumn is when boots really shine. Striding into the spotlight in darkly distinguished leathers, this season's styles combine practicality with elevation and striking good looks. Photography by Jack Webb, styling by Malina Gilchrist.

Booted

A delicious dash of retro on the right, courtesy of these stacked-heel, round-toed ankle boots in tan calfskin by HERMÈS and beige, wine and mustard madras-check flared trousers by GUCCI. On the previous page, the black leather round-toed boots and grey flannel trousers are both SAINT LAURENT by Anthony Vaccarello.

Precisely paired: the black pointed-toe leather boots on the left are by STUART WEITZMAN and are worn with indigo stitch-creased flared wool trousers by LOUIS VUITTON.

Booted

There's something of the frontierswoman to SANTONI's black leather boots with tan leather double-buckle faux half chaps, worn here on the left with grey wool trousers by PORTS 1961.

Stepping out in CÉLINE: the black calfskin *santiag*-stitched mid boots and khaki mohair trousers are both from Phoebe Philo's purposeful autumn collection for the house.

Booted

The black leather pointed-toe ankle boots with crimson lacing by ALEXANDER McQUEEN and the black-and-ecru Prince of Wales-check trousers by MARGARET HOWELL on the left make for a flashy combo.

The hemline of the black wool stitch-creased flared trousers on the right falls exactly at the ankle, showcasing the sumptuous tan leather square-toed boots with white contrast stitching. Both are by LOUIS VUITTON.

Booted

With their robust heels and commanding curves, BALENCIAGA's black leather calfskin platforms are resolutely modern boots. The brown wool trousers are by TOGA. Model: Danielle Korwin at Parts Models. Styling assistance: Gage Daughdrill. Production: Rosco Production.

beautiful
people

NORSE PROJECTS

Rachel Whiteread

Everything Rachel Whiteread, CBE, Turner Prize-winning art-ist, makes is about us: our histories, our lives, our deaths, our absences — cast in concrete. It started with a spoon. Eventually it encompassed a whole house.

At 54, Rachel is working at both scales. Her extraordinary sculptures combine a comforting homeliness with a nightmarish quality. But she is also making quieter "shy sculptures" in remote places. One day she'll make a map of them. For now, a survey show at Tate Britain plots her work from London's Archway Road to California's Joshua Tree National Park. It's a chance to cele-brate the mournful poetry of her monumental take on the world.

Portraits by Nigel Shafran

The master caster

Rachel

When it comes to her art, Rachel Whiteread doesn't compromise. Rather than see her best-known work, "House" (1993), a life-size cast of a family home in east London, moved from the place it was made for, she allowed it to be destroyed after only 11 weeks, even though she regarded it then – and still does now – as "one of the best things I've ever made". She later endured five years of aggressive questioning to get her design for a memorial to Jewish Holocaust victims in Vienna approved without having to alter it. "I'm just like a bull. If I want to do something, I'll keep going until it's done," she tells me when we meet in her studio in early May. Her "pure bloody-mindedness", as she describes it, has made her push her body to its limit for the sake of her art. In 1990, when she made "Ghost", a cast of the living room of an abandoned home at 486 Archway Road in north London, she hauled all the 25-kilogram bags of plaster up the hill to Highgate herself, one by one, on the back of her bicycle. "It was nuts," she says, recalling the effort required.

Rachel achieved critical success early, aged only 25, with her first solo exhibition at the Carlisle Gallery in London in 1988. Since then she has enjoyed sustained acclaim in Europe, the United States and further afield, a feat few artists manage. Her contemporaries Damien Hirst and Tracey Emin – fellow Young British Artists championed by Charles Saatchi in the 1990s – might be better known today, but their artistic output and reputations have ebbed and flowed over the years. Rachel's have never wavered; in her 30-year career, there have been no false steps, no embarrassing misjudgements. She was the first woman to win the prestigious Turner Prize, in 1993, and the first female artist – and the youngest person ever – to represent Britain with a solo show at the Venice Biennale in 1997, when she was 34 (taking the prize for "an outstanding achievement by a young artist").

"Rachel hasn't had periods when her work has not been well received, and that's quite rare," says Ann Gallagher, the director of collections at Tate and the co-curator of an exhibition now at Tate Britain which surveys Rachel's career to date, from the sculptures she made for her debut show to a concrete chicken shed cast earlier this year. This is her first solo museum exhibition in the UK since 2001, when the Serpentine Gallery in London displayed several of her large sculptures. "It seemed the right time," Gallagher tells me. "I wanted to give audiences, especially younger generations, the chance to see what she's produced."

Rachel's studio is in Camden Town, north London, across the road from a guitar shop. Around the corner, there are tattoo parlours and small, independently run cafes. I visit one lunchtime in May. An unprepossessing doorway leads into a garage and then down a staircase into the vast, soaring space where Rachel spends her working days. Light rushes in from windows that line one side of the studio and a skylight that runs the length of the roof.

Rachel moved here two years ago from the East End, where she had lived and worked since the late 1980s, when she was a student at the Slade School of Fine Art. Last year she and her husband, the artist Marcus Taylor, also transferred their home (they have two boys, Connor, 16, and Tommy, 12) from a former synagogue in Bethnal Green to a house close to Hampstead Heath. "We decided we needed to get out of Shoreditch. It has had its day," she says. "I loved it when it was the real arsehole of London. I loved the frisson of it." Gentrification has transformed the streets where Rachel found so much inspiration for her work, and for her "the magic is gone."

As we sit on benches at a long wooden table and sip the cappuccinos she has made, she answers my questions in a thoughtful, circumspect manner. Her responses are brief, and when she feels she's said enough, she simply stops talking, sometimes mid-sentence. She does not enjoy being interviewed – "I just want to get on with my work. I get sick to death reading about myself," she says – and prefers to live her life out of the spotlight. "She is a really famous artist who is hugely respected, but nobody knows who the fuck she is," her friend the artist Gary Hume says. "If you can manage that, as she has, then you're free."

Rachel, 54, is wearing a navy blue tabard by Margaret Howell over a long-sleeved striped cotton top. Howell is one of her favourite designers, she says, and on the three occasions when we meet for this article she is wearing the British brand's utilitarian pieces. "I like clothes that look modest but might not be modestly priced," she says, and laughs. The style suits her: she is down-to-earth, unassuming, with none of the self-importance of some very successful artists. She is short, her stature belying the sheer scale of many of the sculptures she has made with her own bare hands and the materials (dental plaster, wax, concrete, resin, papier mâché) she has manipulated to fulfil a purpose they were never intended for. Her tousled shoulder-length red hair, freckled complexion and tiny silver nose stud ("I've had it since I was 18; it's just me") give her a girlish, youthful appearance.

Rachel was born in Ilford, Essex, in 1963. Her mother, Pat, was a feminist artist, and her father, Thomas, a geography lecturer, then a university administrator. She has older twin sisters, Karen and Lynne. Karen runs the charity Pram Depot, which provides recycled baby clothes and equipment to mothers in need, and is herself an artist. Lynne is an art teacher at a primary school in north London. At times, growing up with twin sisters, Rachel felt like "a bit of an outsider", she says, and would spend hours in her mother's

Text by Cristina Ruiz

studio creating "collages, papier-mâché things, paintings". But she was "always interested in making bigger stuff" too. Her father built two separate studios for his wife and let Rachel help "from about the age of five," she says.

Pat Whiteread was an abstract painter who went on to make mixed media works that explored the degradation of the natural world. (Rachel has a few of her mother's canvases stacked in her studio; "I'm going to put some up at home," she tells me.) In the catalogue for an exhibition she helped organise at the Institute of Contemporary Art (ICA) in London in 1980, she wrote, "All my work reflects my concern with ecological damage which I see as being a consequence of a technological society dominated by males." The show, entitled *Women's Images of Men*, was planned by a group of female artists who met regularly in the basement of the Whiteread home in Muswell Hill, north London, where the family had moved when Rachel was seven. Sandy Nairne, then the director of exhibitions at the ICA (and later the director of the National Portrait Gallery in London), was the only man in the room. "These were strongly opinionated artists," he tells me by phone. "There was vigorous debate about what should be shown and how we would show it until we came to a consensus." Rachel, then a teenager, was at those meetings too. "I would make cups of tea for everyone, then sit at the back of this really smoky room and watch all these slides going up and everyone arguing about everything," she says. "It was completely fascinating."

Despite the artistic household, or perhaps because of it, Rachel chose not to study art until she was in the sixth form. "I went back into it and thought, What a silly ass I've been. Why didn't I do this right from the beginning?" She did an art foundation course at Middlesex Polytechnic before going to Brighton Polytechnic in 1983 and the

Slade in 1985, where she completed a postgraduate degree in sculpture. She remembers those days as an "amazing" time. "There was a great sense of freedom – we had grants, we had money, we had facilities, we had space."

At Brighton she fully embraced the student lifestyle. "I got very, very drunk a few times – I must have nearly killed myself with the amount I consumed. I took drugs, all that kind of stuff. Those were probably my most reckless years, before I met Marcus." (She met him at the Slade. "I was in the second year, he was signing up for the first year, and I always say that I chose him out of the queue. He says he chose me.")

 Rachel studied painting at Brighton, though she tells me she ended up "hanging out a lot" in the sculpture department, where she had her first artistic breakthrough. The sculptor Richard Wilson had driven down from London with "a homemade foundry, a furnace on the back of a trailer," to run a casting workshop. "You'd never be able to do it now," Rachel says. "We were all burning polystyrene, making these terrible toxic fumes, dropping hot metal on our feet. It was all very exciting." Rachel pressed a spoon into sand and then poured liquid metal into the cavity it had made. The resulting cast resembled a spade. "It had lost its spoonness. I remember thinking, 'Wow, that is so simple, but it has changed something so much.' It made me look at the world slightly differently. If you cast the space underneath a bed, it's like a bed, but it isn't a bed any more. It's just a way of making the world slightly strange."

The realisation set Rachel on a path which she pursued with "extraordinary intensity of purpose," the artist Phyllida Barlow, who taught her at the Slade, says. Rachel continued to transform domestic objects like spoons and hot-water bottles, and then, as her technical ability grew, so did her ambition,

Rachel

and she extended her investigations from the objects we use every day to the very spaces we live in.

For "Ghost" in 1990, she spent some 50 days plastering the walls of a Victorian living room (with those 25-kilogram bags she had pedalled from east London all the way up Archway Road), then waiting for the plaster to set, cutting it out in panels and removing them one by one. She remembers the project as "hugely challenging". For one thing, she trapped herself inside her own artwork when she plastered over the room's door and was entombed until the plaster had dried. "It wasn't for long – a couple of hours. For that short period, I felt like a nun," she says. But it wasn't until she had reassembled the sculpture that she fully realised what she had made. Early one morning she went into the studio, and "there was this beautiful pink light hitting 'Ghost', and I suddenly realised that I was the wall. And that was quite a thing." What she means is that in the plaster cast of the room, all its features had been inverted: the fireplace had gone from being a recess to protruding outwards; the light fittings and the door handle had been reversed. So when you look at "Ghost", it is as if you are trapped inside the wall, a silent witness to the space left behind when all the people have gone.

The finished sculpture was displayed at the Chisenhale Gallery in London and then bought by Charles Saatchi (today it belongs to the National Gallery of Art in Washington, DC). Rachel now compares "Ghost" to the Netflix show *Stranger Things*, in which people get stuck in a terrifying parallel reality that overlaps with our own.

When we see Rachel's work, there is a disquieting sense that something is not quite right; she imbues it with emotions such as longing, loss and sometimes even terror. She wants her sculptures to provoke a "sense of unease" in the viewer, she says, by combining "a lovely homeliness" with a "sinister, even nightmarish" quality. There are never any people in her art, but nearly everything she makes is about us: our histories, our lives, our deaths and, finally, our absence.

Take her sculpture "Shallow Breath", made in 1988 for the Carlisle Gallery show. Rachel cast the underside of a single bed; the work's surface was imprinted with the slats which supported the mattress. Her father had died a few months earlier at the age of 59, and the sculpture, which suggests the weight of a human body pressing down on the space beneath, was "a bit of memorial to him," she says.

Abandoned sites have long appealed to Rachel. "As a really young kid in Essex, I would hang out in old Portakabins built on bomb sites after the war." After the family moved to London, she and her friends would break into Highgate Cemetery, sometimes at night, and "terrify ourselves because it was fun". In those days, the cemetery was a neglected, overgrown landscape. "It had been abandoned for quite a long time; lots of the graves had been destroyed or vandalised." (She later returned as a volunteer, "clearing undergrowth, rejigging tombstones and reworking paths".) When she had a studio near the site of the future Olympic Park in Carpenters Road, she would explore disused factories nearby. (Grayson Perry worked in an adjacent space. "She was making moulds underneath chairs," he says by email, "and the thing I most remember was the overpowering smell of resin coming from her room.") "One of them was probably incredibly dangerous," she recalls. "They used to make furs there, and they use mercury for that. I'd go in and crawl around the vats and look at stuff."

After "Ghost", Rachel went on to cast several more rooms and even entire flats. When she and Marcus moved into the former synagogue, Rachel made casts of the rabbi's and caretaker's apartments, three staircases, and the floor of the area where the congregation used to pray. (Tate now owns one apartment and a staircase; the Guggenheim owns the other apartment and a staircase. The remaining staircase and the floor are in private collections.) But she is most famous in Britain for "House", a public sculpture that unexpectedly generated a national debate about contemporary art, electrified the media and was even discussed in the House of Commons.

Unveiled on 25 October 1993, "House" was a life-size cast of a Victorian terraced home at 193 Grove Road in Bow, Tower Hamlets, commissioned by Artangel, a non-profit organisation which places temporary art installations in public spaces. The rest of the terrace had already been demolished to make way for a green space as part of a government regeneration plan. "House" stood as a silent, solitary testament to the loss of working-class communities in east London.

The critics loved "House". The public flocked to see it. But not everyone was enthusiastic. Eric Flounders, the leader of Tower Hamlets borough council, described it as "utter rubbish" and "entertainment for the gallery-going" elite. He spearheaded a campaign to have it destroyed. James Lingwood, the co-director of Artangel, recalls how the work became a "lightning conductor" for wider debates on elitism, regeneration and the place of culture in society. "We could not have foreseen the level of controversy [it generated] and the sound and fury that swirled around it." The irony is that "House" celebrated the very people Flounders represented.

"It gave monumental importance to the lives of people who had come through all sorts of experiences, the war and so much more," Phyllida Barlow says. "It was a glorious monument to London itself."

1994
  Rachel Whiteread has been photographed by Nigel Shafran at intervals throughout her career. This portrait was taken when she worked from Acme Studios' former perfume factory on Carpenters Road in Hackney Wick, east London.

"I'm just like a bull. If I want to do something, I'll keep going until it's done. Pure bloody-mindedness."

2017

When Rachel moved into her north London studio in 2016, she resolved to rid herself of all unnecessary ephemera. A plan chest of drawings were shredded and turned into papier mâché, some of which she cast on sheets of corrugated iron and had framed.

On page 175, Rachel is pictured at her Camden studio on 16 May 2017.

2017

Rachel's studio is decorated with geraniums, which she takes great pleasure in pruning and deadheading. They were grown from cuttings from her late father's plants.

This portrait of Rachel was commissioned
at the time she was creating her work "Untitled
(Floor)" (1994–95).

"I've been lucky to be able to make some tough work and big
work — work that men would find challenging to make."

Rachel

The work had always been intended as a temporary installation, but its supporters had hoped it might remain in situ permanently. Some collectors offered to save it by moving it to another location. But Rachel said no: "House" had been made for the East End, and it needed to stay there. And so, 78 days after it had been unveiled, it also died there. On 11 January 1994, Rachel watched as a bulldozer smashed it to pieces. Her extraordinary sculpture which immortalised the memory of a house had itself become a memory.

After "House" was gone, Rachel had "a moment of mourning", she tells me, but for her, the sculpture endures, perhaps as a reminder that the path to great art is to cleave to one's vision, no matter how ambitious. "When I'm thinking 'Where am I going?' with a particular sculpture, I always think about 'House'," she says. "It has informed so much of my work."

Just two years after its demolition, Rachel found herself under attack again for another public sculpture. In January 1996, her design for the Holocaust memorial in Vienna was chosen unanimously by an international jury. Her proposal was for a concrete room lined with books, their spines turned inwards so you cannot read the titles. The memorial is a testimonial to the intellectual life of the Jewish people who died under the Third Reich and all the books they would have written that we will never read. It was meant to be completed within 18 months, but for five years Rachel was questioned in endless committee meetings through repeated changes of government. "Everybody was really aggressive, asking me, 'What is your memorial? Why does it look like a bunker?' And I would say, 'It's not a bunker, it's a library.'" But she always knew that it did indeed look like a bunker, perhaps hinting at Austria's failure to fully acknowledge its role in the atrocities and to deal with persistent anti-Semitism. "I wanted to make something tough. I worked really hard to get the design past them, and I did." At one point she threatened to pull out when it was suggested that the sculpture be moved to a different site, Heldenplatz – Heroes' Square. "I refused to let it be anywhere other than Judenplatz," she says. When the monument was unveiled in October 2000, there were snipers on nearby rooftops in case of protest by supporters of the far-right Freedom Party, which was then in the ascendant. "The whole experience was terrifying," Rachel says.

The controversies surrounding "House" and her Jewish memorial in Vienna were "extremely difficult", Rachel tells me. She had "a bit of a breakdown" afterwards and was "very, very anxious for a while". Although she continued to produce major sculptures – in 2005, for example, she filled the cavernous Turbine Hall at Tate Modern with "Embankment", a landscape of white plaster casts of boxes inspired by the experience of sifting through her mother's belongings after her death – she remained sensitive to charges of misusing public money. Indeed, when she accepted the commission for the Fourth Plinth in Trafalgar Square, she did so knowing that she would have to self-fund the work. "Monument" (2001), a transparent resin copy of the plinth placed upside down on top of the original, was paid for through sales of a limited-edition of 15 maquettes of the sculpture.

Rachel has an ambivalent relationship with the art market. In 1988, her first exhibition at the Carlisle Gallery included casts of the inside of a wardrobe (covered in black felt) and the underside of a dressing table and the space inside a hot-water bottle, and "Shallow Breath". An art dealer she declines to name offered to buy all four pieces. But he also wanted exclusive rights to purchase everything Rachel made for the next five years. "The offer was incredibly exploitative, and even though I was extremely skint, I said no." With extraordinary prescience, she kept all four sculptures herself. For the first time since 1988, they are on display together at Tate Britain.

"I'm just not interested in how much things are worth," Rachel says. She is nevertheless represented by powerful galleries – Gagosian in London, Luhring Augustine in New York, Lorcan O'Neill in Rome – which sell her small works on paper for between $12,000 and $14,000 and her larger sculptures, such as specially commissioned concrete sheds, for about $500,000. Although she knows that the market still discriminates against women and that if she were a man she could sell her work for more, it doesn't seem to bother her. "How much money do people need? Personally, I've been very lucky to be able to make some really tough work and big work and work that men would find challenging to make."

One of the artists she most admires is the American Richard Serra, a notoriously intimidating artist whose massive abstract sculptures in sheet metal are hugely challenging to make, move and install. She tells me a funny story about first meeting him at a private view in New York after "House" had been unveiled in London. "He pointed across the room and said, 'Get that Rachel to come and talk to me.' And I was like, 'You come and talk to me.'" And he did. (She met another of her heroes, the late abstract painter Agnes Martin, in Venice in 1997. "She came and saw my show at the Biennale, which was a joy. It was like meeting the Queen but more interesting.")

Rachel's move to her new studio in 2015 prompted a massive clear-out. (When she happens upon a reality television

Rachel

show about extreme hoarders trapped in their homes by decades of junk, she thinks, "Oh no, that could have been me.") The studio is now filled with displays of her small metal sculptures. There are many casts of spoons, the utensils that played such an important part in her artistic development. She lets me hold one as we talk; it is a weighty, seductive thing which recalls the object it was made from but also its absence. Even this small, simple sculpture has a spectral quality to it. Phyllida Barlow says it is as though "a ghost of something is being trapped and caught in its moment of disappearing. The object's loss becomes the sculpture. It is beyond beauty; it is sublime."

Other pieces have been cast from items Rachel has found, such as discarded soft-drink cans and plastic bottles flattened by traffic. As part of her reckoning with her own rubbish, she took the vast quantity of paper that had accumulated in her old studio – sketches, magazines, letters, accounts, invitations to private views – shredded it, and turned it into papier mâché. Her drawings decorate the walls.

Rachel has only one assistant, who works in an office upstairs. It wasn't always so. At one time she ran two studios – one for sculpture, the other for drawings – staffed by a team of employees. "I was becoming the producer of my own work rather than actually making it myself any more. I wanted to go back to basics." And so in 2005, after completing "Embankment" for the Turbine Hall, she got rid of most of her staff and now answers to no one but herself, spending her days drawing and making papier-mâché sculptures while listening to BBC Radio 4 or podcasts. One of her recent favourites is *S-Town*, a murder mystery of sorts that tells the story of an eccentric horologist in rural Alabama. "It was absolutely brilliant. I drew and binge-listened for two days."

She is still making monumental sculptures. When we meet, she is getting ready to install a work commissioned for the new US embassy in Nine Elms, south London, which is scheduled to open later this year. Her piece, a concrete cast of a pre-assembled flat-pack house, will straddle the embassy's public entrance – half the sculpture will be on the wall inside, the other half outside. "In the 1950s, all of the houses in America were prefabricated," says Rachel, whose sculpture serves as a neat metaphor for the American dream of economic success and home-ownership that is the ideological foundation of the country.

Away from the spotlight, Rachel has enjoyed making what she calls "shy sculptures" in remote places. There are casts of an old boathouse on a fjord in Norway ("The Gran Boathouse", 2010), a hut in Norfolk ("Houghton Hut", 2012), two sheds – "Shack I" (2014) and "Shack II" (2016) – in Joshua Tree National Park in southern California and a concrete cabin on Governor's Island in New York ("Cabin", 2015). These works, she says, are as much "about the journey of seeking them out" as they are about experiencing the sculptures in person. Rachel hopes to make more of these "shy sculptures" and one day publish a book and a map for hardcore fans.

For these larger works she collaborates with a former assistant she has known since the Slade who runs his own foundry. Many of Rachel's closest collaborators have a long history with her. Before organising the Tate show, Ann Gallagher curated three other exhibitions of Rachel's work, including her Venice Biennale display 20 years ago. Rachel's friendships are long-standing, too. "I really made a decision when I first became famous that I wanted to keep my core group of friends. Those sorts of friendships are very special. They live deep in your heart."

Whiteread

The week after our interview, on a sultry evening in Rome, I meet several of these friends at an exhibition of Rachel's new work at Galleria Lorcan O'Neill. At the centre of the show, a pair of heavy, ice-blue transparent doors made of resin ("Due Porte", 2016) leans against the walls. They were cast from doors recovered from the building in which we stand. "Rather than getting rid of them, I sent them to Rachel," Lorcan O'Neill says. The surface of the doors is pristine, with no imperfections; they recall the pared-down purity of minimalist art. It's an effect Rachel has achieved through years of trial and error. "It's very, very difficult to cast resin in that size with no bubbles," O'Neill says. The effect is extraordinary. It is as if Rachel is able to view the world with X-ray vision, seeing the simplest architectural structures as transcendental, timeless things of beauty.

Nearby, sections of a papier-mâché chicken shed create an entirely different effect. Where the resin doors are hard, the shed is soft, its textured surfaces speckled with multi-coloured remnants of Rachel's rubbish. Papier mâché is the material of children's school projects, the material she made small objects out of in her mother's studio. Her return to it suggests she is mining her own memories, recreating the world by channelling the limitless imagination of a child. Rachel is showing the shed to Ann Gallagher.

Later, on the gallery roof, lined with lemon trees, dinner is served for a small group. An early boyfriend of Rachel's, Steve Trent, is here. They went to school together in Muswell Hill and have known each other since they were 11 (today he

runs the Environmental Justice Foundation in London). Rachel Wyndham Wincott, an accountant, also met Whiteread some four decades ago. "Rachel's friends now are her friends from then, and that is a key to who she is," says another friend, the artist David Batchelor, who is married to Ann Gallagher. This group reunites for birthdays, anniversaries and every exhibition opening of Rachel's. "I sent her a text on my way saying I felt quite weepy that we were all going to be together again," Wyndham Wincott says. "There is proper love here; it's family," she adds. Seeing Rachel tonight, drinking wine under the stars and exchanging memories with her dearest friends, I feel as if I am seeing her for the first time as she really is.

Today Rachel is celebrated the world over for the mournful poetry of her sculptures and for her capacity to distil the essence of the most difficult subjects. "There is an innate dignity and gravitas to her work," Grayson Perry says. The accolades, which began early in her career, are still coming. In January, Rachel accepted the International Medal of Arts from the US Department of State, awarded to artists who "have helped define America's cultural legacy through their artistic excellence". The prize is for her sculpture in Nine Elms. When I ask about the honour, she is quick to point out that she accepted it from President Obama. "I got the medal in the last days of his administration. If it had been Trump, I would not have taken it. Please put that in capitals."

The work is still coming, too. Earlier this year, her design for a Holocaust memorial in London, at Victoria Tower Gardens, a public park next to the Palace of Westminster, created in collaboration with her husband, Marcus, and the architects Caruso St John, made it on to the project's shortlist (the result will be announced this autumn). The proposal consists of a translucent life-size cast of a nearby Victorian memorial commemorating the abolitionist Thomas Fowell Buxton, surrounded by smaller casts of the same monument. Light flows through the sculptures, illuminating an underground chamber where visitors will hear accounts by Holocaust survivors.

Like so many of her works, Rachel's London Holocaust memorial would capture the ghosts of lives past. She doesn't believe in actual ghosts, although she believes that people do see them. "They exist in your mind. That's what they are: hallucinations." But she does think that buildings have a life of their own, that somehow they may be imprinted by the lives lived within them. "I do have a sort of funny sense with buildings," she says. "A couple of years ago we stayed in a stately home in Cornwall, and I found it incredibly creepy. Being in the kitchen on my own, it didn't feel right – like there was something there, a feeling of unhappiness. And one night I felt like I saw something out of the corner of my eye. Then I thought, For God's sake, get a grip."

24/7

The fascination of double denim lies in the minute disparities between many almost-identical versions. Here are seven.

Photography by Paul Wetherell
Styling by Max Clark

This year A.P.C. celebrates 30 years as purveyor of the most dashing denim. Here, Xiaomeng Huang wears the French company's notably handsome faded-indigo Brandy denim jacket and its New Standard jeans, also in faded indigo, with blue denim ankle boots by DRIES VAN NOTEN.

There are 10,000 possible PIN code permutations, the most popular being 1234 and 1111. Ayaana Aschkar Stevens is wearing a vintage acid-washed denim jacket by LEE, Farah skinny jeans in faded indigo by AG JEANS, and a black cashmere polo-neck jumper by MM6 MAISON MARGIELA. The bag is vintage and the boots are by DRIES VAN NOTEN.

Owing to its popularity in North America, a three-piece denim outfit is known as a Canadian tuxedo. Here, Ayaana wears a vintage Western denim shirt from CONTEMPORARY WARDROBE, a vintage 1970s FIORUCCI embroidered denim waistcoat, a black cashmere polo-neck by MM6 MAISON MARGIELA, and dark denim jeans with cut-off hemline by DIOR. The black leather shoes are by CHURCH'S.

The comforting whirr of the cashpoint is in fact artificial, solely there to confirm that the money is on its way. Xiaomeng stands by in a blue cotton-and-linen Western shirt and blue skinny jeans, both by SAINT LAURENT by Anthony Vaccarello, a vintage black plastic belt with bottle-top decoration, and black leather Chelsea boots by CHURCH'S.

On bright days the sun's glare can be bothersome. Emily Jones leans in wearing a vintage denim blazer from MIU MIU's late, lamented menswear line with stonewashed cropped jeans by MM6 MAISON MARGIELA and black leather loafers by CHURCH'S.

"Free Cash" — is there ever really such a thing? This dark blue jacket in bonded raw denim by STELLA McCARTNEY can be taken to the bank, though. The black cashmere polo-neck jumper is by MM6 MAISON MARGIELA, and the blue skinny jeans are by POLO RALPH LAUREN.

CALVIN KLEIN was doing designer denim before the term was even coined. Ayaana is wearing an indigo denim shirt with red contrast stitching; high-rise, straight-legged indigo denim trousers with red contrast stitching; and bordeaux Western leather boots — all by CALVIN KLEIN 205W39NYC.

Models: Ayaana Aschkar Stevens at Premier Model Management, Xiaomeng Huang at Viva Model Management, Emily Jones at Select Model Management. Hair: Matt Mulhall at Streeters. Make-up: Joey Choy at Streeters. Photographic assistance: Sam Wilson, Paul Allistair. Styling assistance: Louis Prier Tisdall. Production: Rosco Production.

Pictured at the Mulleavy sisters' home in Pasadena, California, Laura wears a white cotton ruffled shirt from RODARTE's collaboration with & OTHER STORIES.

Pasadena

Laura Mulleavy

and

Portraits by Clara Balzary

Pasadena

Kate Mulleavy

of Rodarte

Portraits by Clara Balzary

Kate is wearing a white cotton ruffled shirt from RODARTE's collaboration with & OTHER STORIES and gold butterfly earrings from RODARTE A/W '14.

Inseparable sisters Kate and Laura Mulleavy have made a powerful film about being lost in the woods, but as fashion designers the pair have always trodden a single-minded path. For more than a decade, their home-spun, high-end fashion house, Rodarte, has bucked the aesthetic and commercial norms of our times, albeit with enthusiastic support from an army of superfans including Anna Wintour and Michelle Obama.

Now, after leaving New York Fashion Week behind, the Mulleavys are Americans in Paris, the spiritual home of haute couture and art-house cinema. It's the culmination of their every California dream.

Text by Mark Smith

It rarely happens, because they're usually in the same room, but some months into the writing of the screenplay for their debut feature film, *Woodshock*, which opens in US cinemas this month, Kate Mulleavy received a telephone call from her younger sister, Laura.

Kate: "She called me up and she said..."

Laura: "I think we're kinda fucked here."

The reason for the apparent crisis was something Laura had just read in a book – a film theory tome that's a perennial on the reading lists issued by the more prestigious film schools.

Laura: "We'd never directed a movie, so we'd bought some books on the craft."

Kate: "And I got lazy, so I said to Laura, 'Why don't you read them and just give me the synopsis, the CliffsNotes.' So she does, and she gets to this part in one of the books where she's like..."

Laura: "*Wait a second*. Because this book is explaining how one of the great tropes of filmmaking is to show a man walking along the banks of the Seine in the middle of the night, deep in concentration and lost in thought. And then the author – this highly respected film guru – says, 'But obviously this kind of treatment could never work for a female character.' And I'm like, *Excuse me*!"

Kate: "So, she calls me and she's like, 'Well, we have a problem because...'"

Laura: "Our entire movie is about watching a woman think!"

Kate: "It's all that happens!"

Kate and Laura both talk at a brisk California clip and deliver sentences in a sort of psychic relay race – the chops, changes and interpolations are frequent and mind-boggling. The timbres of their voices are usefully distinct, though. Laura sounds a touch more sing-song San Fernando in her inflections, and affirms statements by saying "todally". Kate's voice is a shade deeper,

17

more confidential, and her speech is dotted with helpful signposts. She's all, "Here's the situation," and "To put things in perspective to you…" and "If this makes sense to you…" And it typically does.

Although Kate and Laura aren't strangers to the world of film – they have made shorts to accompany several of their collections – they had never before made a feature film. And yet their entrée into filmmaking is reminiscent of the curious fashion folk tale that started them on the road to where they are today.

When I meet them in late June, they are in Paris, contemplating the "logistical insanity" of their debut couture week presentation for their brand, Rodarte, having previously shown in New York. French couture's governing body – demonstrating what it calls its "international influence… and openness to fashion's new frontiers" – has been relaxing its rules to attract the likes of Rodarte and fellow American brand Proenza Schouler, ready-to-wear guest members whose practice shares something of couture's dedication to sartorial craft. Not that Kate and Laura go in for furbelows themselves. Sitting amid the greenery of the Hôtel Amour courtyard in the 9th arrondissement, both dressed in blouses, jeans and ballet pumps, they look chic, sunny and straightforward – a world away from what international *Vogue* editor Suzy Menkes calls the "unknown danger" of their lavish, darkly ethereal catwalk creations.

Kate scrolls through the forthcoming schedule on her phone (a device she and Laura used to share). They've got an edit of their show ("They're actually *really* pretty," Laura says, as if the 47 looks could have gone either way) and a model casting with the veteran Jennifer Venditti. These are followed by meetings with their show director of 10 years, Alexandre de Betak, and Michel Gaubert, the sound director for brands such as Chanel and Louis Vuitton. "Everyone we work with is really fun," Laura says. "We can't deal with working with not-fun people."

Born in 1979 and 1980 respectively, Kate and Laura are prime examples of the Xennial microgeneration who've spent their working lives online but are old enough to have lived a childhood free of the internet. "The whole time, we were either playing together in the woods outside or we were reading," Laura says of their early years in Aptos, northern California. "One way or another, having free time meant being in an imaginary world." They both describe their experiences of natural landscapes, in particular the ancient redwood trees that bordered their back garden, as the sentimental education that defines them. As Laura puts it, "Every creative process is different, but ours is one of intertwined sense memories.

I feel so lucky that we had a childhood that continues to nourish us creatively to this day."

William Mulleavy, a mycologist of Irish extraction and now the CEO of Rodarte, and his wife, Victoria, a Mexican-Italian artist whose anglicised maiden name was Rodarte, relocated to Pasadena, north-east of Los Angeles, when their daughters were teenagers. Both Kate and Laura remember being torn between dedication to their studies and their mother's alternative syllabus. "She'd say to us, 'You should take a week off school and I'll show you all the Hitchcock movies!'" Kate says. "I think we benefited in so many ways from having such open parents. Literally, the only rule was that we weren't allowed to get married before getting a college degree."

Both sisters went to the University of California, Berkeley, where Kate read art history and Laura read English literature. Their academic paths crossed for just one 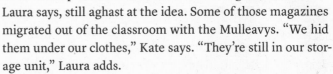 day, when they both started a course in costume design before swiftly ditching it. "They wanted us to cut up these 1960s and 1970s *Vogues*," Laura says, still aghast at the idea. Some of those magazines migrated out of the classroom with the Mulleavys. "We hid them under our clothes," Kate says. "They're still in our storage unit," Laura adds.

After graduating, the sisters moved back home and holed up watching movies for a year – largely horror films. They also plotted a trip to Italy. As Laura would later tell the actress Natalie Portman in *Interview* magazine, "Both of us have really obsessive personalities, and we overplanned it so much that we cancelled it." The money saved for that trip and the proceeds from the sale of rare records (including a first pressing of the Velvet Underground's debut album) amounted to $16,500 – sufficient to produce a California redwood-inspired collection of seven dresses and three coats and take it to New York in January 2005 on the advice of their friend Cameron Silver, the owner of Decades vintage store in LA. Within days, *Women's Wear Daily* had featured the clothes on its cover, under the headline "Starlet Chic". This apparently piqued the interest of Anna Wintour, who visited the Mulleavys in LA three weeks later and famously furnished them with one piece of advice – to always keep what they do "personal".

Kate embarks on the story of Rodarte's first runway presentation for Autumn/Winter 2006-7 at New York Fashion Week. Neither sister had attended a fashion show before, let alone orchestrated one, but Kate felt strongly that the process of creation would be incomplete without rigorous documentation. Accordingly, the sisters enlisted their friend Autumn de Wilde, an emerging photographer who had taken portraits of West Coast musicians including the late indie singer Elliott Smith, to accompany them

Laura and Kate

to New York as they performed something of a headless chicken routine, calling up model agencies and blithely asking for their most famous models, to no avail. "We were nobodies!" Kate laughs at the memory.

Two days before the show, "Autumn says, 'You guys just don't know what you're doing! I'm calling my friend Shirley, who's a stylist in LA.' So this woman called Shirley Kurata gets on a plane the night before our show, having never met us before."

Kurata was immediately taken by the couture-like details. "The first look was a dress with beautiful organza flowers running down it," she says. Now Lena Dunham's stylist, Kurata has worked on every Rodarte show since. "I'm so glad I flew out there to lend a hand." And De Wilde continues to follow the Mulleavy sisters around the world, populating Rodarte's Instagram account with behind-the-scenes imagery while compiling an archive of photography. "Sometimes I feel like our shows are just an excuse for all our friends to come together and have great parties," Kate says.

Rodarte became a fixture on the New York show schedule – and on the backs of Keira Knightley and Michelle Obama. The press was almost uniformly enthusiastic; Mary Tannen of *The New York Times* described an early collection as "exquisite to the point of pain". The Mulleavys won a clutch of awards, including CFDA Womenswear Designer of the Year in 2009. Commercial collaborations with the likes of Gap suggested that Rodarte might be open to widening its appeal. When Pierre-Yves Roussel, the acquisitive chief executive of the French luxury goods conglomerate LVMH, was seen in the front row at its Autumn/Winter 2010–11 show, the rumour mill went into overdrive. But in the end, nothing came of it.

That same February Rodarte's first solo exhibition, *Quicktake*, opened at the Cooper Hewitt museum in New York.

As well as admiration, it prompted the start of a recurring strain of Rodarte criticism – that the Mulleavys' highly conceptual, artisanal approach to clothing might condemn the brand to being little more than a museum piece itself. For now, at least, Kate and Laura would continue down the road less travelled.

"Woodshock" is a real term, Kate tells me. "It's a colloquialism for what happens when you get totally lost in a forest and start making decisions which cumulatively lead to something really bad." *Woodshock* the film starts with its protagonist Theresa, played by Kirsten Dunst, killing her mother by administering a powerful cannabinoid drug. Morally, things only get murkier and more subjective from here, as Dunst delivers a verbally sparse but astonishingly nuanced representation of grief, regret and isolation, all set against the fast-depleting forests surrounding Eureka, a town on northern California's redwood coast.

Eureka is known for two things apart from its genius name: its role in the West Coast lumber trade and its latter-day status as the administrative centre of Humboldt County, where it is estimated that a quarter of all income comes from marijuana cultivation. Cast and crew spent 30 days embedded in this strange, Venn-diagrammatic subculture at the edge of a national forest in July and August 2015. There were two directors' chairs, as you'd imagine. "Everyone wondered how it would work," Laura says, "but all the actors told us it was like being directed by one person. We just tried to convey our directorial viewpoint in the cleanest and most supportive way." Kate adds, "We were meticulously prepared before the shoot in terms of knowing our subject matter. Plus we're very intuitive when we work together, so I think we both felt confident that in the moment, if the other

one needed to speak out, it would be the right thing. We didn't have to confer endlessly."

Famously, the sisters contributed the distressed tutus used in the 2010 ballet horror film *Black Swan* after Natalie Portman, who had worn Rodarte to premieres, described their work to the director, Darren Aronofsky. "I think we were so aligned with him artistically because he loved the same things about the ballet as we did," Laura says. "He loved the idea of the ruined toe shoe over the perfect one. Like us, he could see that inside the extreme beauty of ballet there were also grotesque aspects and dysmorphia." Kate talks of film as "the modern art through which Laura and I try to understand ourselves."

As a protagonist, *Woodshock*'s central character, Theresa, is tricky in pretty much every sense, and Dunst has spoken of the role as the toughest of her career to date. A long-term friend of the Mulleavys, she's been wearing their clothes on the red carpet for years – most memorably in 2014 when she turned up at the Met Gala in a black silk gown emblazoned with the Death Star, from Rodarte's *Star Wars*-themed capsule collection. She committed to *Woodshock* early on – Kate and Laura wrote with her in their collective mind's eye – and she serves as the film's executive producer. "I had complete faith in Laura and Kate because they work so hard and they care so much," Dunst says by email. "Together we were dedicated to making something very special and meaningful to us all."

Gloriously, the film's script has the rare distinction of having been partly written at the Ritz – or at least what used to be the Ritz-Carlton in Pasadena, before it was sold to the Langham Hospitality Group in 2008 and rebranded accordingly (the new name hasn't stuck). Kate refers to the 392-room Spanish Colonial

Revival-style pile at the foot of the San Gabriel Mountains as "this little hotel near our house" – their house being a 100-year-old redwood building. When they were on a roll, they'd rent a guest room rather than return home.

Woodshock is distributed by A24, the independent company behind *Amy*, *Spring Breakers* and *Moonlight*, last year's winner of the Oscar for best picture. Noah Sacco, the head of acquisitions at A24, recalls meeting Kate and Laura at a coffee shop in New York's NoMad district in early 2013, when A24 Films, as it was then called, was a promising upstart indie distributor that was taking risks on unknowns as well as those with advertising and fashion experience. "We'd been working with directors like Sofia Coppola, Jonathan Glazer and Harmony Korine," Sacco explains over the phone. "There's a certain deliberateness of vision with those filmmakers, and I felt that in the DNA of Kate and Laura's vision there was the same sort of authorial spirit – a real appreciation of craft." He was not, he says, concerned by their lack of experience. "Here were two very sophisticated artists operating on a very high level creatively," he tells me. "It seems to me that the medium in which they choose to operate is a secondary factor."

Charlotte Cotton, a British curator who has worked at the Los Angeles County Museum of Art and is now doing a project with LA's Metabolic Studio called Bending the River Back into the City, says Kate and Laura's way of working is recognisably Californian. "They are strongly aligned with all manner of creative practice that goes on here," she tells me. "LA has the best constellation of art schools in America, plus it's relatively affordable to live and work here, so you have a lot of young, creative people who form their networks early on, then remain as part of a very supportive community."

Certainly, in the age of work-anywhere mobility, it's easy to see how people might be drawn to the West Coast, with its endless sunshine, scenery and healthy food culture, over cold and corporate New York – particularly as Madison Avenue cedes its clout to Silicon Valley. Hedi Slimane, the photographer and former creative director of Saint Laurent, who moved to Los Angeles in 2011, recently explained his decision to The Business of Fashion. "LA felt like the most vibrant and relevant observatory at the time. Why not design from here and define an aesthetic around California?" he said. "Finally the fashion industry followed three years after. Everyone loves LA now." For their part, Kate and Laura are delighted that their locale seems to have a new currency in popular culture – although they do have some geographical quibbles about the opening sequence of *Big Little Lies*. "We really need to talk about the fact that all those driving shots are in Big Sur, not Monterey!" Laura says. "Well, it's Carmel, really. We will educate the world!"

A single West Coast project would seem to sum up their overarching ethos. In 2011, for their first book, *Rodarte*, Kate and Laura engaged the services of two art photographers they admire. Catherine Opie was invited to photograph her friends – some of whom were in the Mulleavys' circle, some not – wearing knitted and macramé Rodarte designs, which would be printed opposite images by Alec Soth, who had been given a map of California marked with the sisters' most cherished locales. "He came back with pictures of the *exact* parasitic plant that had inspired our loose knits," Kate says. "It was a map of our subconscious through Alec's eyes, and a very cinematic idea." Laura still gets a kick from reading the negative reviews on Amazon. "People were like, 'This isn't a fashion book,' and we're like, 'Well, what is it, then?' We worked with two incredible photographers to try to express what all of these clothes actually *mean* to us. We like stories. That's just who we are by nature. We were never going to be like, 'Here's our perfume ad with some girl lying on a bed in her underwear.'"

Certain fashion commentators have also been critical of Rodarte, interpreting the label's continued focus on artisanal craft and collaboration as some sort of hapless failure to launch. "What's confusing to people, perhaps, is that Rodarte's importance in fashion has not been matched by the scale of their business ambition," Sally Singer, US *Vogue*'s creative digital director, tells me. "Whenever anyone decides against taking outside investment and scaling up, it's always seen as a refusal to play the game."

"Look," Kate says, "we're in an environment where there are billion-dollar luxury conglomerates, and they make amazing product. I'm a big fan of lots of different people working in that way, but we're a tiny, independent company. I want what I make to have meaning, and the truth is that for that to happen in our particular case, the work has to come directly from us."

These days there are typically no more than five people working alongside Kate and Laura in their LA studio. Kate and Laura tell me that their post-Paris markets meetings have been the healthiest yet. That said, they admit that their fondness for intricate beadwork and time-consuming constructions means that pretty much any Rodarte showstopper balances on a knife edge in terms of profitability. "Ooh, remember that time we hand-marbled the leather instead of just printing it?" Laura asks Kate. "The problem is that I can see the difference, and I'm always going to choose the more beautiful option."

Even so, there are changes afoot. After 12 years of showing in New York, Rodarte's application to the Chambre Syndicale de la Haute Couture for a place on the official Paris couture week programme – which was accompanied by a letter

Kate Mulleavy

"We're a tiny, independent company. I want what I make to have meaning, so the work has to come directly from us."

Laura Mulleavy

"Everyone wondered how it would work, but all the actors told us it was like being directed by one person."

Laura and Kate

The Mulleavys' garden features a lush array of plants, such as the copper-orange Bettina rose, pictured here. A climbing hybrid tea, it can reach 4.5 metres in height.

In pages 202–203, Kate wears a white point d'esprit blouse with pearl buttons from RODARTE's S/S '17 collection and gold earrings, as before, with her own jeans. Laura is in a white Chantilly lace blouse and gold lily earring from A/W '17.

Hair: Nikki Providence at Forward Artists. Make-up: Samuel Paul at Forward Artists. Photographic assistance: Robbie Corral. Production: Rosco Production.

of personal recommendation from Sidney Toledano, the chief executive of Christian Dior Couture – was accepted, and the Mulleavys were given a slot on the first day of the schedule in July. "I think we have the purest reasons for wanting to show here," Laura tells me. "We're not pretending to be haute couture in the strictest sense – I mean, we don't work out of Paris and we don't follow all those rules. But we do make between one and 20 pieces of each piece that we show, and we work with artisans to make them. We may be in a weird hybrid space between ready-to-wear and couture, but we feel strongly that we're a match here."

While they're at pains to say how grateful they are for all the support New York Fashion Week and the CFDA have afforded them over the years, they've grown used to being regarded as what Laura terms "the odd duck in town" – an accomplished but somewhat baffling proposition amid the athleisure and all-American glamour. On witnessing Rodarte's presentation in the lush gardens of the 16th- century cloister at Port-Royal abbey hospital, I think it's fair to say that the intricate, artisanal wares are having their swan moment, and the reviews have been almost universally positive. "I don't think our approach has changed fundamentally," Kate tells me after the show, "but I do think a lot of the reaction is that the context allowed people to understand the work. It's as if Paris has helped people to *read us*." When a couple of weeks later Céline Dion – the unofficial mascot of this season's Paris couture week – appeared in an embroidered floral jumpsuit, sequined cape and snake booties by Rodarte, alongside looks from Chanel and Valentino, in a camp video commissioned by US *Vogue*, it felt like a joyous affirmation of Rodarte.

There is commercial potential in the relocation, too. Paris couture week is where orders for the world's most lavish wedding dresses are typically placed. And Rodarte's presentation – a pastel-hued collection shown on models with hair haloed in gypsophila – has undeniably bridal overtones. Importantly, couture week's January and July show schedule means retail orders will be able to live in store for longer than if they were shown during the four-season ready-to-wear calendar.

Increasingly, the Mulleavys seem to be segmenting their business in imaginative ways. Last year Kate and Laura moved into e-commerce, selling accessories and their popular "Radarte"-emblazoned sportswear – first seen in a line Rodarte did for Opening Ceremony in 2011 – straight to consumers via their own website. At the time of the launch, Laura said, "It's a cool way of speaking directly to the fans of the brand and giving them things that are asked for. It's not something we normally get to do." With its fun, punny name and bleachy tie-dyes, the Radarte line is an acknowledgement that the artisanal stylings of their

catwalk collections simply can't be watered down successfully, and a nod to the surf-and-skater subcultures of Santa Cruz, the northern California beach town creepily immortalised in Joel Schumacher's 1987 vampire movie, *The Lost Boys*. As children, Kate and Laura were enraptured by the sartorial kaleidoscope of the town's famous boardwalk. "There were Hare Krishnas, people taking tons of acid, and very straight-laced people," Kate says. "I think that's where Laura's and my love of fashion started – from seeing all these different people, all dressed completely differently." Despite the international reach, it's important for that global online fan base to feel Radarte is coming from somewhere specific.

Kate and Laura have visited Paris plenty of times in the past but profess to be "terrible" at navigating the city and its language. Still, within minutes of sitting down and ordering eggs with ham, they've demonstrated a working knowledge of the history of Haussmannisation that gave the City of Light its broad boulevards and cafe culture, gone into raptures over their shared love of Proust, and furnished me with a sightseeing tip. "You *have* to visit the palaeontology pavilion at the natural history museum," Laura says.

Kate: "First of all, it's an amazing old arcade with intricate ironwork. And inside, there's the work of these two incredible 18th-century naturalists. They've set out the skeletons with the smallest at the front, so it looks like a stampede. My favourite thing."

the
cocktail needle

As if cocktail hour could be made any more glamorous an expanse of drinking time, a brand-new invention arrives. This autumn The Gentlewoman gets together with the jeweller Delfina Delettrez to introduce the cocktail needle — the exquisite pick of the divine and the dissolute.

Photography by Blommers/Schumm

Ever since olives were introduced to martinis in 1920s America — possibly to mask the taint of the Prohibition gin that was then their principal ingredient — the aim has been to skewer the slippery fruit with a tool equal in style to the suave drink it accompanies.

With the help of Delfina Delettrez Fendi, the solution has been found: a sleek rhodium-plated stainless-steel needle, embellished with either a pearl (seen here), a green agate, or a blue or pink chalcedony in its turning sphere. Delicious.

207

the gentlewoman

While one olive is considered classic, up to three will fit along this needle's 11.5-centimetre shaft. Connoisseurs advise leaving them alone until the drink is finished, so the olives absorb maximum alcohol, but our instinct is, of course, to pick the needle up. Adding the jewel-studded turning sphere gives the drinker something else to play with, Delfina says.

With four limited-edition styles available to buy from Delfina Delettrez and The Gentlewoman shops from 6 October 2017, you could collect the set and start a drinking game. Cheers!

delfinadelettrez.com
thegentlewoman.com/shop

back-flipping

gold-winning
ever-smiling

Portraits by Alasdair McLellan
Styling by Jonathan Kaye

Simone Biles

Oh, that winning smile! On this page, Simone is wearing a pink jersey three-quarter-length-sleeved polo shirt with cat appliqué by MIU MIU.

In the opening spread, she wears a green jersey bodysuit with three-quarter-length sleeves by GUCCI.

No one who watched the Rio Olympics will forget the astonishing acrobatics of the sunny four-foot-eight powerhouse gymnast from the USA. Simone Biles captured hearts and minds (not to mention a great many medals) at the 2016 Summer Games, somersaulting into the sporting stratosphere as the star-spangled poster girl for a new era of gymnastics. But for all her game-changing virtuosity, Simone is a down-to-earth 20-year-old from Texas with a natural gift of the gab.

With Tokyo 2020 on the horizon, she is setting her sights on Olympic glory once again, but at least for now, Simone's attentions are more focused on the serious matters of dancing, shopping and Zac Efron.

Simone

For as long as she can remember, Simone Biles has begun the year by writing down her goals. Like any gymnastics-obsessed girl growing up in suburban Houston, Texas, her ambitions were fairly circumscribed: to do better in school, master a new skill in the gym, grow a bit taller. Over time, as her precocious power and explosiveness began to set her apart as an elite junior, her list grew to include graduating to the senior ranks, placing in the world championships, making a magazine cover or two, and representing her country in the Rio 2016 Olympic Games.

This January, having surpassed all but one of her goals (despite her wishful thinking, she's remained 1.43 metres tall since she was 13), including winning the Olympic gold medal for individual all-around champion, Simone broke with tradition. "I didn't write down anything," she tells me when we meet for lunch in New York in June. "It's my year off. I didn't want to think about anything other than relaxing and being with friends and family."

Nice, in theory. Since vaulting her way into the public consciousness last summer in Rio by winning four gold medals (and a bronze) and becoming the most decorated American gymnast ever (14 World Championship and five Olympics medals and counting), Simone, 20, has had quite the year. She's met her idols Beyoncé  and Kim Kardashian, visited the Obamas before they left the White House, appeared in a music video for teen-bait Jake Miller, hit the red carpet in a seemingly endless parade of custom-tailored frocks, and traversed America in an exhibition tour of 36 cities with her "Final Five" Olympic teammates.

"She's always at an airport," says her best friend, Rachel Moore, a former gymnast. "I don't know how she does it, but as soon as she's back, she's not the type to just crash. She'll be like, 'Hey girl, wanna hang out?'"

In between hitting Forever 21 ("Hello, the mall is not going to shop itself!") and getting her nails done with friends, Simone has signed with Octagon – one of the world's most respected sports agencies, which represents Michael Phelps, among others – and with a host of sponsors, including Nike. Her pre-Olympics net worth was estimated at $2 million, but her competition success and relatability with a key young demographic make her highly marketable to the mass audience that gymnastics attracts. "Simone's athletic accomplishments alone place her in a very rare class of athletes in terms of market value," her agent, Janey Miller, says.

 Simone has also published a memoir, *Courage to Soar*, and was named one of *Glamour* magazine's Women of the Year alongside Patrisse Cullors, Alicia Garza and Opal Tometi of Black Lives Matter, Miuccia Prada and Christine Lagarde of the International Monetary Fund. In news that might not sit well with Simone's beloved Kardashians, she launched her own emoji app, called – naturally – Simoji. The poppy graphics, which she curated, include leotards and gold medals aplenty as well as insider nods like a sticker of Simone, an Olympian-level napper, catching some Zs. "I slept in the cab coming over here," she informs me.

Simone is in New York for a couple of days, having flown in from Los Angeles, where she's been living for the past few weeks while competing in *Dancing with the Stars*, the American version of the British television show *Strictly Come Dancing*. DWTS, like *Strictly*, features a broad church of celebrities. (This season's eclectic lineup of competitors ranged from has-beens such as Mr T to young stars like Normani Kordei from the American pop group Fifth Harmony.) After a shock elimination in the semi-finals, Simone and her partner, the Australian dancer Sasha Farber, finished off the podium, coming in fourth. Filming wrapped the week before our meeting, but the wounds are still fresh. "Sasha and I were so sad," Simone says, with the newly minted dolefulness of someone unaccustomed to losing. "I really thought we could win."

It's blisteringly hot outside, but Simone is dressed in head-to-toe black Nike gear, including a cropped hoodie that covers her strikingly muscular arms (a small tattoo of the Olympic rings she had done on her right forearm after Rio is just visible). She has ombré extensions in her naturally straight hair, which she is wearing loose rather than in her customary ponytail; her fingernails, manicured into prim French tips when she's competing, are today shellacked in a sparkly taupe. When a waiter approaches our table, she orders the mini steak frites (charmingly mispronouncing "frites" as "frights"), then taps away nervously on the table with her nails. She notices me observing her fidgeting and confirms what her friends had told me: she's "very OCD".

Beyond extending her reach to a wider audience, the DWTS experience was meant to be a fun diversion for Simone, who was homeschooled from the age of 13 so she could focus on gymnastics and missed out on teenage rites of passage such as proms and school dances. She had never danced with a boy before going on the show ("I was terrified the first day of practice," she confesses) and could scarcely walk in heels, let alone dance in them.

Simone fared well from the outset, scoring high marks (but not perfect 10s) for her foxtrot, samba and rumba, yet the judges complained that she was too robotic, didn't focus enough on character and story, and, depending on the week, smiled too much or not enough. By quarter-finals night,

Text by Horacio Silva

she had clearly had enough of the feedback. When the co-host Tom Bergeron asked why she hadn't smiled at some of the judges' compliments, Simone answered with the now infamous burn "Smiling doesn't win you gold medals."

"Ugh," Simone exclaims, in her go-to expression of disgust, when I mention the uproar that followed on social media. "You get it in gymnastics too – 'Work on your facials, smile more.' We look mean a lot of the time because we're concentrating so hard. If you don't, you get hurt."

I point out that despite her efforts to try something new, with *DWTS* she still trained all week, stepped out in rhinestones and received scores after each performance. "Yeah, but at least in gymnastics the judges know how good I am," she bristles, widening her eyes and pursing her lips. I suggest that Carrie Ann Inaba (a pop singer turned dancer who, alongside Jennifer Lopez, was one of the Fly Girls troupe on the 1990s TV show *In Living Color*) was particularly hard on her. "Everyone in the show has a judge that's a little bit tougher on them," Simone says. "But Carrie Ann wasn't having it – any of it! She said I was too perfect when I dance. Can you believe that? I trained 14 years of my life to be perfect. Ugh."

29

30 In 1976 the Romanian gymnast Nadia Comăneci, the first person ever to score a perfect 10, on the uneven bars, dazzled audiences at the Montreal Olympics with an otherworldly single-flip dismount off the balance beam. Simone routinely performs two. Her signature move in the floor event, "the Biles", involves a double backwards flip executed while maintaining a difficult, unstable mid-air position called a layout in which the body is fully outstretched. To complicate matters, Simone somehow adds a half twist towards the end of the tumbling run, so she lands blind, with her feet facing forwards. She is the only woman capable of doing the move.

Simone, who is stockier than many of her competitors, is built for power and speed – a huge advantage in an evolving sport that values daring athleticism above the safe balletic grace of past champions like Comăneci and the Belarusian Olga Korbut. "I have been criticised for my body, but if I didn't have this build, I wouldn't be able to do what I do," Simone says. "Everyone wants this prototype of a skinny girl with the perfect butt and legs. I just don't get it. It's not Build-A-Girl.

"We are all built differently," she continues, "and we all know that there are elements of what we do that are influenced by our body type. We understand that and learn how to substitute for it. If you are more muscular, you have to work on elegance a bit more. If you are long and elegant, you have to work on your power a little more."

Because of the power Simone is able to generate off the ground in the vault and floor routines (her favourite and highest-scoring  31 events), she is able to clear more than double her height (higher, even, than some of the men, who are considerably taller and stronger), giving herself time to perform more complex skills in the air. "I know exactly how difficult that move [a full-twisting double-back dismount off the beam] is because I worked so long and so hard on it," Shannon Miller, who won gold with it on the beam at the 1996 Olympics, told a reporter just before the Rio Olympics. "When Simone does it, you just get so jealous because she just floats."

After decades of dominance by the Russians and Romanians, the sport had appeared to reach its physical limits with the emergence of powerful gymnasts like the Americans Mary Lou Retton in the 1980s and Simone's idol Alicia Sacramone in the early 2000s.

Simone

But the old scoring system rewarded technical precision over risk. In 2006, a complicated new open system was introduced which did away with the fabled perfect 10. In its place, judges would now offer two scores: one for execution (worth up to 10 points) and the other for difficulty (technically limitless, though only the top eight skills are counted per routine), which are then combined. ("To be honest, we're all still a little confused by it," Simone's Final Five teammate Laurie Hernandez tells me by phone.) Impenetrable to the uninitiated, the new system places a premium on difficulty, amply rewarding the courageous. It's why Simone is able to make the rare error in competition – as she did at the 2015 World Championships in Glasgow, where she almost fell on the balance beam and stepped out of bounds on floor – and still win by wide margins.

But it would be a mistake to attribute Simone's ascent simply to the revision of the scoring code, says Rhonda Faehn, the head of the women's programme at the governing body USA Gymnastics. "I genuinely feel that Simone would have been able to adapt to any code in any era and have as much success, if not more," Faehn tells me. "Sure, her vault and her beam dismount are the hardest in the world and potentially worth a lot of points, but she executes them so beautifully, with a form that's really hard to fault."

While most viewers, whose interest in gymnastics is usually limited to the Olympics, might not be able fully to comprehend how Simone is pushing the limits of physics with moves that build on classic elements, they have connected with her personal narrative. If Simone is tired of covering old ground in every interview, she hides it well. "As I've got older, I realise that my story is my story and if anyone is going to tell it, it should be me," she says. "I was so young when everything happened, and you're not really processing

much as a three-year-old, but I am who I am because of it."

Simone Biles was born in Columbus, Ohio, as the third of four children. Her mother, Shanon Biles, struggled with addiction to drugs and alcohol, and from the age of two Simone was in and out of foster homes, along with her siblings, Ashley, then nine, Tevin, five, and Adria, six months. (Her father abandoned the family early on.) When Simone was five, she and Adria

were adopted by their Texas-based maternal grandfather, Ron, who had been in the US Air Force before becoming an air-traffic controller, and his second wife, Nellie Cayetano Biles, who owned a nursing home. (Simone's siblings Ashley and Tevin were adopted by Ron's sister, Harriett.) After an initial stint of calling her grandparents "Hammom" and "Hampa" (she couldn't pronounce the Gs at the beginning of each word), Simone has referred to them as her parents. Ron, 68, and Nellie, 63, now own World Champions Centre, the gym where Simone trains.

Simone's home situation seemed so normal to her that she assumed everyone's was the same. She recalls being at the gym when she was about 10 and inadvertently revealing to her friends that she and her sister were adopted. "It was a shocker," she says. "No one knew. We were sitting in a circle and somehow the subject came up. None of my friends knew what adoption was, so I told them what had happened to us. How crazy is that? First, that they had never heard of it, and second, that I thought everyone was adopted."

Simone was six when she was introduced to gymnastics, after a school field trip was cancelled because of a heatwave. Her teacher took the class instead to Bannon's Gymnastix, a private club that offers children's tumbling and gymnastics classes, where Simone

mimicked what she saw some of the other children doing. Nellie immediately signed her up for a tumbling class. "She was already jumping and flipping all over the house and was very athletic," Nellie says. "The boys at school used to challenge her to a race or an arm-wrestle, and she would beat them."

Aimee Boorman has been Simone's coach since Simone was eight years old, and she was the head coach of the American women's team at the Rio Olympics. A former gymnast and now a co-owner and the head of women's gymnastics at the EVO Athletics facility in Florida, Boorman recalls seeing Simone for the first time after being tipped off about the new girl at the gym. "She was born for this," Boorman says. "The way she carried herself, she didn't look like your average six-year-old. And the fact that she couldn't sit still was so appealing. You could just tell that she wanted to do more and more." Though Boorman recognised Simone's precocious talent, she and Simone's parents decided not to push her. "It was going to be up to her how far she wanted to go. We were just waiting in the wings, waiting for her to say, 'Yeah, let's go.'"

The decision to commit to gymnastics full-time and be homeschooled was difficult on the gregarious teen. But Boorman kept the gruelling training sessions fun and encouraged Simone's clowning around at the gym. It's a lighthearted approach to her sport that Simone has maintained. "When we're in routine mode, she is incredibly focused and serious," Hernandez says. "But when we're in between rotations or in the gym working on skills, she's a total goofball. She makes everybody crack up all the time."

Boorman considers Simone's ability to switch from joker to killer mode – cheering on and jesting with her teammates one minute and attempting the near impossible the next – to be a competitive advantage. "Other athletes shut off the world to get in the zone," she says.

Biles

"We look mean a lot of the time because we're concentrating so hard. If you don't, you get hurt."

Simone wears a black wool raglan sleeved jumper by RAF SIMONS and black Pro Hypercool training tights by NIKE. The belly button stud, worn throughout, is Simone's own. On the previous page, she is wearing NIKE's black Indy logo sports bra and the black training tights.

Simone

The four gold and one bronze medals Simone won at Rio are the heaviest ever — at 500 grams each, they are 10 times the weight of those awarded in Athens 1896. Here, Simone is wearing a gold brass "S" pendant over a black T-shirt, both by CÉLINE.

"That makes Simone more nervous and unfocused, so she stays in her silly, supportive space for as long as possible until she has to step up to do her job – and then it's game on. She's a natural competitor."

Like many great athletes, Simone is not particularly interested in overthinking her talents or her serendipitous introduction to the sport. "I really do believe everything happens for a reason," she says. "You can only do what God has given you the opportunity to do, and He opened the doors for me to do this."

A practising Catholic, she attends church every Sunday with her family and lights a candle for her safety before every meet. Over the years, she has learned to be more of a proselytiser. "It's such a personal thing," she says, "and I get that people don't want to be hit over the head, but kids nowadays see me, or LeBron James or Cristiano Ronaldo or whoever, and they think that we are just born with this talent. But it takes an army for us to do what we do, and for some of us, faith is a big part of that. As you get older, you realise that if something is important to you and helps you get through things, then it's good to let others know."

After her medical records were released last September in the wake of the cyberespionage group Fancy Bear's hacking of the World Anti-Doping Agency's database, Simone took to Twitter to reveal that she has attention deficit hyperactivity disorder (ADHD) and has been granted an exemption by the International Gymnastics Federation to take Ritalin, posting, "Having ADHD, and taking medicine for it is nothing to be ashamed of, nothing that I'm afraid to let people know."

Today, she says, "If you know me or have seen me at all, it's pretty obvious that I have ADHD. So what's the big problem? I'm practically bouncing off the walls most of the time. It really didn't bother me, but I thought it was important to speak out and tell kids that it's OK to have ADHD, that you can go far in sports and in life. It doesn't have to hold you back from anything."

On social media she shares not only amusing intimacies, such as a recent video of herself under the influence of happy gas after the removal of her wisdom teeth, but also the sacrifices she has had to endure in her quest for gold. "We look all dandy out there," Simone says, "but as soon as we get out at 6pm, we are limping out the door." Though she is not big on the cryotherapy treatments or cold compression machines some of her peers opt for, she spends countless hours after training in her NormaTec recovery boots, which squeeze and release her legs to get the circulation going – so long, in fact, that the boots have their own emoji on her app. "It's a dirty little secret, but once you reach a certain level, you end up spending a fortune to keep your body in one piece."

She talks about how lonely she was being homeschooled ("Even an invisible friend to talk to would have been nice") and how she has her fair share of bad days. "Like every kid, I went through a bratty period. I've had failures, too. Even though you don't see them on TV, it doesn't mean I don't have them." And she wants young girls to know that it's fine to have a body as ripped as hers. "It's perfectly OK to have muscles and be stronger than some of the boys," she says. "When you're young you tend to want to follow the crowd, but you're your own person at the end of the day, and that includes looking a little different to everyone else.

"Social media can make you look so bad or so good," she adds. "And I think kids look at that and think, She is so perfect, nothing bad ever happens to her."

Simone suggests walking off our lunch. She says she is surprised not to have gained any weight since the Olympics. She'd like to keep it that way. "Even five pounds makes a dif-  ference. With what we do in the air, you can really tell," she says. "I haven't been to the gym in months, but the training for *Dancing with the Stars* was intense, so I can cheat a little bit and order something other than salmon. So much salmon."

We head towards Central Park. Before we are even out of the door, Simone is approached by a young fan for a selfie. She graciously obliges and assures me that she is not worried about being accosted on the street. "At this point I'm used to it," she says. "It doesn't stop me from doing what I want to do. Plus, I get it. I had this dream and I went after it, and the whole world got to watch me doing it. So now they want a piece of me. As long as they're respectful, I don't mind."

As if to test her patience, within seconds, a middle-aged woman stops Simone at a pedestrian crossing and asks to take a photo. Simone poses for one picture, then another, and is remarkably calm in the face of the woman's gruff instructions to move to the side a little and not look at the camera. Oh, and would she mind smiling? It's so awkward and imposing that I feel like letting out an "Ugh" on her behalf. "It happens," Simone says good-naturedly. "Some people think they own you because they have seen you on TV."

We continue towards the park, stopping at every turn for her to indulge her admirers. When a couple of women approach, lean in conspiratorially and tell her, "You should have won," referring to *DWTS*, a huge smile flashes across Simone's face. "They know what's up," she says with a giggle.

We are on the lookout for a boutique that might stock petite sizes, because Simone is "always in the mood to shop". She admires the way young celebrities such as Zendaya, Selena Gomez and Vanessa Hudgens dress, but, she says,

Simone

"I can't wear certain things because of how my body is shaped. I haven't found a specific brand that fits my entire body, but certain places fit me better than others, more than actual brands, so I'm always on the hunt." She has always been told to wear sparkly things, but lately she's been gravitating towards unadorned styles, so as not to draw too much attention to herself.

Fashion is just one of the many things she wants to learn more about on her year off, she tells me after we give up walking in the sun and stop for ice cream. She wants to see more of the world, and spend more than the night or two in each place she typically spends when touring. She loves Belize, where Nellie is from and where the family holidays, but destinations such as Bora Bora, Tokyo, Santorini and Australia are calling her name.

Then there's the tricky business of adulthood – "It's a work in progress," she says – and the changing nature of her relationship with her parents now that she is transitioning into a different life and beginning to go on dates. "I feel like, if anything, we are even closer now," she says.

"It's definitely different and a little weird, but obviously I respect my parents' rules. It's their house; I understand that," she adds. "When it comes to dating, I get what my parents' expectations are. They know what I look for in a guy, too" – a fun personality, manners, and hopefully eyes like Zac Efron, in case you're wondering – "and that I would never bring anyone home to meet them that they wouldn't be proud of." For her parents' part, Nellie tells me later, their main concern is that Simone will have difficulty taking a back seat in life and in relationships. "She has to learn that life is a give and take," Nellie says, "and that you don't have to win every time."

As to what goals she may set herself for next year, Simone says the 2020 Olympics are definitely her main priority. "Athletes get high off competing in big events, and once you've had a taste you just want to keep going," she says. "As soon as the Rio Olympics were finished, I was like, I want to go to the next Olympics."

She is in no rush to return with the audacious new moves she was regularly landing in practice before taking a break. "No, sir," she says, sounding like a true Texan girl for the first time since we met. "The sport of gymnastics is a crazy place to be in. Making up a new skill is almost dangerous at this point, and doing something in training is very different than doing it in competition repeatedly under pressure. It's easy to get injured that way."

Once, in 2013, Simone performed the double double – a double-twisting double-tuck dismount from the beam that has never been performed in competition – and she has video to prove it (more than three million views on YouTube).

Her coach had suggested to Simone that she had enough height to squeeze in the extra twist, and Simone shot back, "Bring out your camera, because I'm only doing it once, and if I die I want it recorded."

Laurie Hernandez suspects that her friend may well be tempted to create some new signature moves once she's back in the gym, but, she says, "Simone didn't leave much room for improvement after the last Olympics. Just to maintain that level is enough because she is so far ahead of everyone else. She is at the very top of the mountain."

Whatever Simone ends up committing to paper for next year, one gets the sense that no one will be forcing her hand. "Even at this age, people want to set goals for me before I've had a chance to set them for myself," she says with barely restrained incredulity. "It doesn't make sense to me. As I like to say, 'Are you doing the sport or am I?' Who is walking the dog here?"

37

"It's perfectly OK to have muscles and be stronger than some of the boys."

Simone got her tattoo in March. She was accompanied by the singer-songwriter Jake Miller, who documented her inking step by step on Twitter. Simone is wearing a black Shape Zip sports bra by NIKE.

Hair: Didier Malige at Art Partner. Make-up: Francelle Daly at Art + Commerce. Manicure: Gina Edward at Kate Ryan Inc. Set design: Gerard Santos at Streeters. Photographic assistance: Lex Kembery, Matthew Healy, Simon Mackinlay. Styling assistance: Fan Hong, Sanna Fried. Hair assistance: Ledora Francis. Make-up assistance: Takahiro Okada. Production: Pony Projects.

The navy-and-white polka-dot silk top by BALENCIAGA and the black-and-yellow print bias-cut silk Elsden dress by DIANE VON FURSTENBERG make a languid pairing. Here, the Dutch model Tessa Bruinsma wears them with a blue, white and gold Infini ring, also by BALENCIAGA, and a 14-carat yellow-gold Ballerina bracelet by CATBIRD.

busy

Patterns are plentiful in the unpredictable months. From crêpe de chine cover-ups to light jersey blouses, how to put it all together is entirely down to point of view.

Photography by Oliver Hadlee Pearch
Styling by Emilie Kareh

An abstracted offering from that master of minimalism, GIORGIO ARMANI, in a coral, blue and white printed silk top with shirring details and loose-fitting embroidered black velvet trousers. Here, Milena Litvinovskaya wears them with a hammered 14-carat yellow-gold Classic ring and 14-carat yellow-gold Sleeping Beauty stud earrings, both by CATBIRD.

I beg your pardon: Milliana Maalim's rose-garden ensemble contrasts a single-stem bloom with a full-blown flowery bower, pairing an almond Velvet Rose printed mohair jacket with Impressionist Garden mohair trousers. Both pieces are by GUCCI, as is the black leather belt with brass buckle. The multicoloured Ex-Libris en Cravates silk twill scarf is by HERMÈS, and the vintage pink-and-black floral-pattern sock boots are from CONTEMPORARY WARDROBE. The Panthère necklace, in yellow gold with emeralds, diamonds and onyx, is by CARTIER.

Milena shows off the rib-knitted cashmere sleeves of the twillaine shirt by HERMÈS, which attach to a silk body in a pink-and-chalk Les Mains print. She is wearing it with yellow-and-cream cat-print jersey trousers by MIU MIU, a vintage green plastic belt by WILLIE WOO from CONTEMPORARY WARDROBE, brown leather Regent Chain loafers by MULBERRY, brown tights by FALKE and a 14-carat yellow-gold necklace with opal teardrop by CATBIRD.

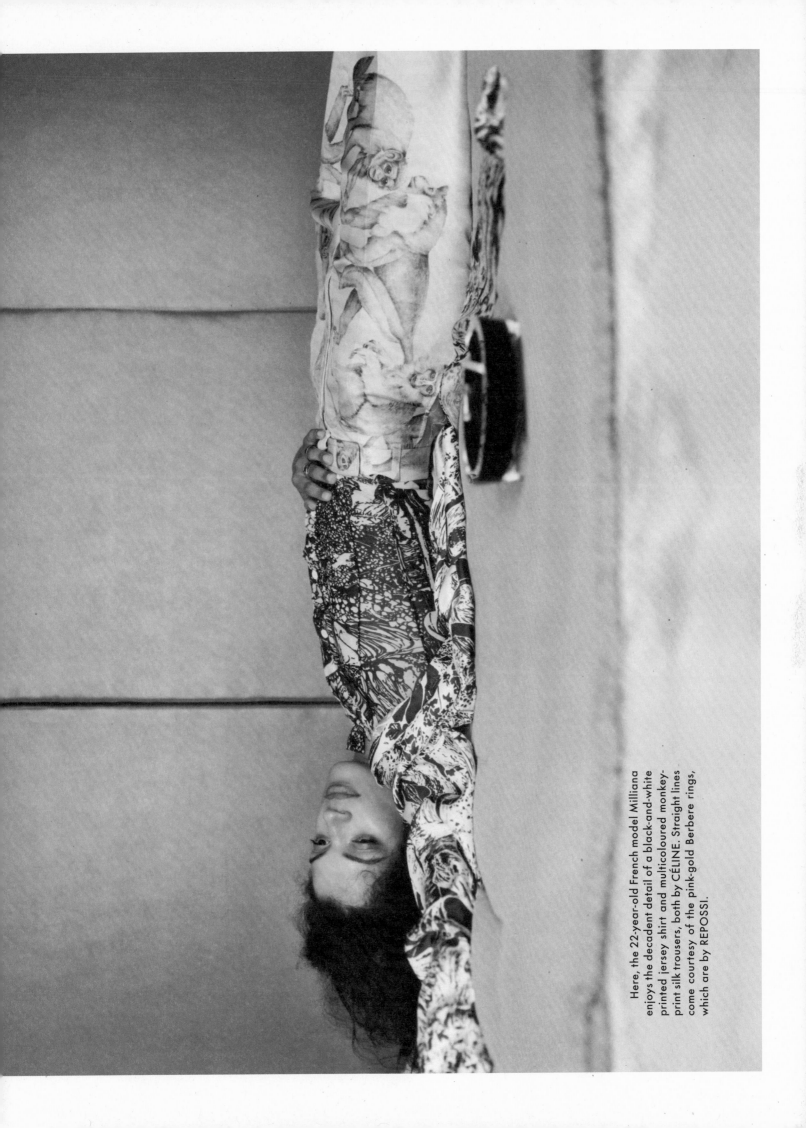

Here, the 22-year-old French model Milliana enjoys the decadent detail of a black-and-white printed jersey shirt and multicoloured monkey-print silk trousers, both by CÉLINE. Straight lines come courtesy of the pink-gold Berbere rings, which are by REPOSSI.

Checks balanced: red, white, blue and black printed silk blouse by MSGM and grey checked wool trousers by TOGA. The rouge nappa leather boots with enamel heels are by ROKSANDA.

Skyscraper heels on beige calfskin boots by ERIKA CAVALLINI, also seen on page 232, are the final punctuation mark in a long look comprising a short-sleeved, multicoloured Rocket print silk top by CHRISTOPHER KANE under a pale green floral-print Delia crêpe de chine dress by ERIKA CAVALLINI. Tessa wears it cinched with a swift calfskin Etrivière belt by HERMÈS.

With a gathered waist and hemlines, the billowing plissé pleats of the Kelani trousers by ROKSANDA make them ideal for hanging in. Here, Russian beauty Milena wears them with a multicoloured striped Hacienda stretch bodysuit by TOPSHOP UNIQUE, brown tights by FALKE, and brown leather loafers by MULBERRY.

The bold pink-and-black stripes of the printed velvet trousers by PUCCI balance to perfection the chequerboard tessellations of LOEWE's pink-and-white patchwork Waffle dress with black leather straps.

Models: Tessa Bruinsma at Next Management, Milena Litvinovskaya at IMG Models, Milliana Maalim at Girl Mgmt. Hair: Cyndia Harvey at Streeters using TIGI. Make-up: Thomas de Kluyver at Art Partner. Manicure: Ama Quashie at CLM. Set design: Suzanne Beirne at D+V Management. Casting: Adam Hindle at Streeters. Photographic assistance: Jack Day, Arther Williams, Rafik Greiss. Styling assistance: Camille Marchand. Hair assistance: Cat Wyman. Make-up assistance: Thomas Waite. Production: Rosco Production.

Gloves indoors? Milena's no slouch. Here, she wears a multicoloured velvet pair from CONTEMPORARY WARDROBE with a green Mikado print cotton top and a multicoloured floral print skirt with feather trim, both by PRADA. The 14-carat yellow-gold Big Hoop Dreams earrings are by CATBIRD.

Making it big with Martine Rose

When Martine Rose, 37, started her company in 2007, menswear was a sea of preppy suits with dandyish pocket squares. Fast-forward a decade and she's coaxed the fashion world into her marvellously voluminous trousers, the hit of her joyfully utilitarian collections. Taking the best from 1980s and '90s subcultures with a dash of Uncool Dad mixed in, Martine is setting new standards through her own-name brand and the Balenciaga men's line for which she consults. And with the introduction of female models on her catwalk this season, women's fashion can look forward to equally broad horizons.

Photography by Andrea Spotorno, styling by Tamara Rothstein
Text by Susie Rushton

"This jacket is huge!" Martine says approvingly of her leather cover-up from Autumn/Winter 2015–16, a collaboration with BEEN TRILL. She's always liked capacious clothing. Her degree collection was "very sculptural, oversized. Nothing body-conscious." Underneath, she wears vintage ADIDAS track pants and a BALENCIAGA men's Spring/Summer 2018 T-shirt with the slogan "Think Big!" "Very apt," she says, eight and a half months into her second pregnancy. The trainers are by NIKE.

The soft, slightly slumping tailored jacket is from Martine's S/S '18 collection, which was shown at the Stronghold Climbing Centre in Tottenham Hale, London. As usual, the soundtrack was of paramount importance. "I told my friend Sasha [Crnobrnja] of In Flagranti, who did the music, that I wanted synthy, dad music. I wanted it to feel slightly Phil Collins-y." Martine's badge, from A/W '17, is in imitation of the kind that might be given out at a conference, she says. The black cotton T-shirt is from MARTINE ROSE A/W '16.

Hair: Mari Ohashi at LGA Management. Make-up: Gemma Smith Edhouse at LGA Management. Photographic assistance: Nicholas Riley-Bentham. Styling assistance: Camille Marchand.

Martine Rose

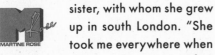

"There are a few reasons I got into fashion, but Michelle was one of them," says Martine Rose of her much older sister, with whom she grew up in south London. "She took me everywhere when she was a teenager and I was a baby. It was like having a younger, cooler mum." This was the 1980s and Michelle Rose, a fan of reggae and lovers rock, wore Hamnett, Gaultier and "amazing Pam Hogg dresses in really bright colours with funny puffed sleeves". Martine also idolised her cousin Darren, whose uniform was Boy London. "He was into acid house, the whole '89 rave scene. I just wanted access to that world. But it wasn't until much later that I identified it." By "it", Martine means the instantly recognisable dress codes of a style tribe.

Over the past decade, as Martine Rose has become the toast of the London fashion industry, those same tribes — plus punk DIY, ravers and '90s bike couriers — have influenced her designs. But she doesn't simply cut and paste references. The extreme silhouettes of Martine's signature pieces, like the supersized trousers and her hunchbacked tailored jackets, come from an interest in proportion play that began when she did her foundation year at Camberwell College of Arts. Then there's her fascination with commonplace characters and the real-life dressing she sees on the street. Martine's repetitive use of logos, sporty outerwear and tweaked tailoring is drawn from her preoccupation with Everyman types, who might be City bankers but lately are more often "dad-y" types, as she puts it. On proud display in her studio in Tottenham, north London, are news photos of Jeff Goldblum and Jeremy Corbyn in cargo shorts and pulled-up sports socks. An image of the latter plus bicycle made it onto her Spring/Summer 2018 show invitation.

"Jeremy's a human being," she says. "I do think he'll be prime minister, though I don't for one second think he'll get it all right."

The non-specific type of menswear these "dads" inspire is so appealing that, for many seasons, women have been buying and wearing it too. Leaning against a rail of clothes from the S/S 2018 collection, dressed in a vintage T-shirt and Adidas track pants, curly hair piled on top of her head, Martine herself is like the cheerful sister anyone would wish to have — relaxed, dry-witted and calm, despite her mounting responsibilities. She's pregnant and due any moment (her first child, a daughter, is two); she's in the middle of applying for two major fashion prizes, awarded by Andam and LVMH; and most pressingly, she has orders to produce from the latest, roundly admired autumn collection, "which we've been scrabbling to meet," she admits.

As if that weren't enough, Martine is also acting as a consulting designer for the Balenciaga menswear collections at the invitation of the brand's creative director, Demna Gvasalia. The pair met in Paris for the first time more than a year ago. "I'm a very informal person," Martine says, as we find a table in the cafe of Tottenham's Bernie Grant Arts Centre. Demna asked Martine if she would be part of his plan to reinvigorate Balenciaga's menswear. She agreed, she says, because the two designers "got on really well. For me, it was the fact that I really, really liked him. Also, I'm Georgian Orthodox, too. I had to convert when I was asked to be godmother to the daughter of a Georgian friend. I went there on holiday last summer. Anyway, Demna found that whole thing insane."

Balenciaga is her first proper job, she says, and it's been a long, almost entirely self-funded journey here from art school and then fashion college at Middlesex University. In between,

there was a small T-shirt brand, LMNOP, run with Tamara Rothstein — now her stylist — followed by shows supported by Fashion East and NewGen, and then

solo presentations in London. In the early days, Martine also worked shifts at Blacks members' club in Soho. "Ten years is a long time to keep chipping away at something before it becomes commercial, but that wasn't really what interested me about fashion. I've never been a businessperson, thinking of what people are going to buy."

Despite her dedication to work, Martine's personal life hasn't suffered. She describes big, frequent gatherings of family and friends, "always with billions of kids", held across south London or at her home in Bethnal Green, east London. Her parents — her mother, Sonia, is a former nurse and her father, Clifford, an accountant, and at one time a Black Panther — have always supported her unquestioningly, as has her partner, a plasterer, whom she met, in a true coup de foudre, outside the LMNOP studio 13 years ago. "The building had scaffolding on it, and he shouted down at me. Something really irritating. I was in a stinking mood that day, and I remember thinking, Ugh, fuck off. Then I looked up and saw that he was quite fit. I was trying to get a big roll of pattern paper into the car, and he swung down from the scaffolding to help me. I was a little bit impressed by that." He's audacious, then — enough to wear her clothes?

Martine thinks for a second. "Not the wild pieces," she says. "Not the triple-waistband trousers. But the tamer pieces, yes."

> "Girls like the wide-legged styles. Some fold from a 60-inch waist into a 30-inch — those accommodate bottoms and hips."

The handwritten Martine Rose label was introduced in S/S '14. "If only it was my own handwriting — mine is atrocious. The logo is a Frankenstein version of a beautiful name label sewn into a vintage army piece I found on Portobello Road. This is my interpretation." Martine still likes Portobello Market, but only on a Friday morning. "It's the one part of London that isn't changing — Golborne Road, Goldhawk Road."

"This fits over the bump perfectly." Martine wears a T-shirt with a decorative "cock ring" from her A/W '16 collection, and ADIDAS track pants. "I think it's absolutely rubbish," she says of the idea that there are clothes for different times of the year. "I remember people saying, 'Ooh, a bomber jacket in spring!' I don't understand the idea of a winter wardrobe and a summer one. Who can afford that? And who wears pastels in summer and black in the winter?" Not Martine. Here and on page 242, the trainers are by NIKE.

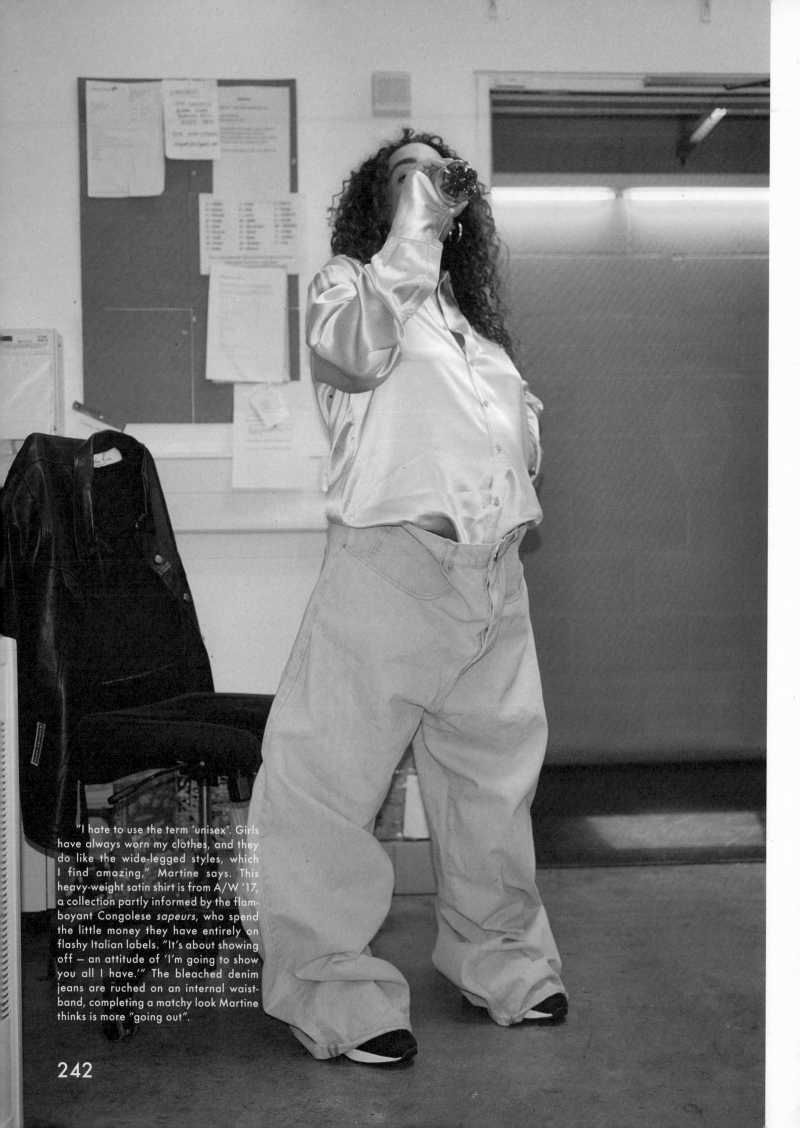

"I hate to use the term 'unisex'. Girls have always worn my clothes, and they do like the wide-legged styles, which I find amazing," Martine says. This heavy-weight satin shirt is from A/W '17, a collection partly informed by the flamboyant Congolese *sapeurs*, who spend the little money they have entirely on flashy Italian labels. "It's about showing off — an attitude of 'I'm going to show you all I have.'" The bleached denim jeans are ruched on an internal waistband, completing a matchy look Martine thinks is more "going out".

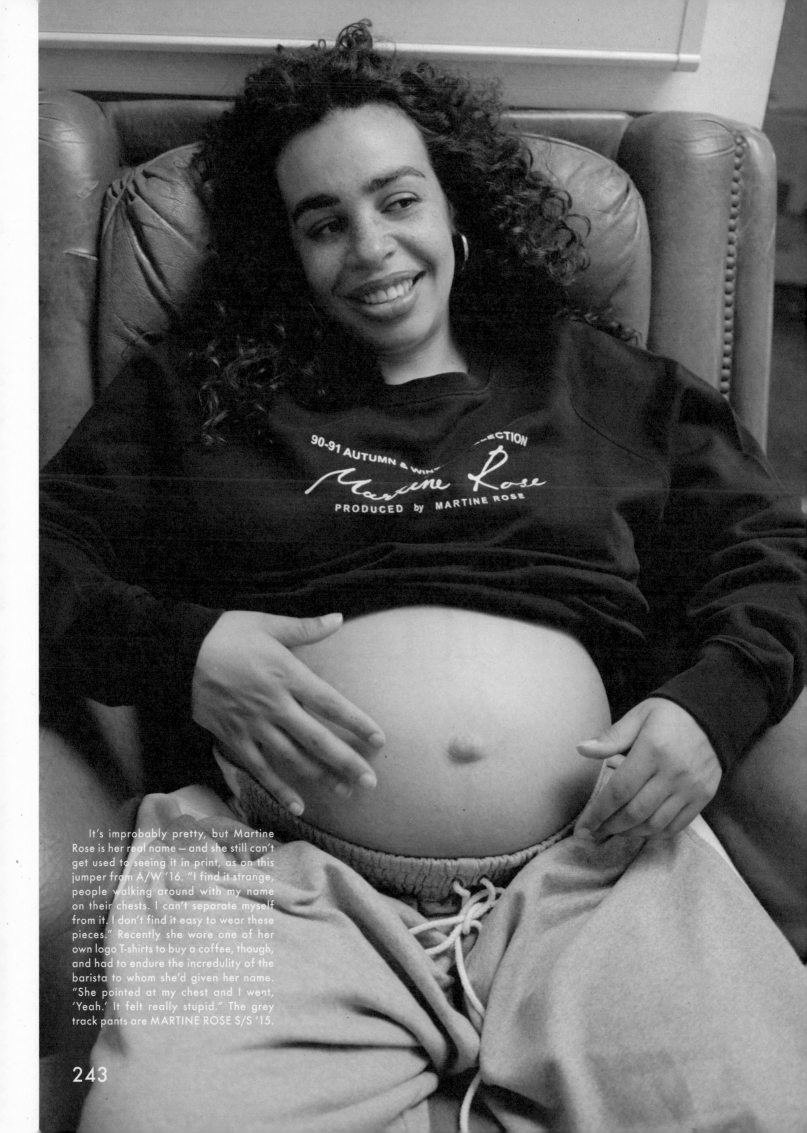

It's improbably pretty, but Martine Rose is her real name — and she still can't get used to seeing it in print, as on this jumper from A/W '16. "I find it strange, people walking around with my name on their chests. I can't separate myself from it. I don't find it easy to wear these pieces." Recently she wore one of her own logo T-shirts to buy a coffee, though, and had to endure the incredulity of the barista to whom she'd given her name. "She pointed at my chest and I went, 'Yeah.' It felt really stupid." The grey track pants are MARTINE ROSE S/S '15.

243

Marcie Mayer

holds the future of Greece in a nutshell

Portraits by Bruno Staub

Marcie Mayer

On a Cycladean island, an American has done a remarkable thing. Marcie Mayer, 53, has taken Kea's mighty acorn from its little oak trees and turned it into gold, using old methods – tanning – and new ones – award-winning acorn cookies.

At a time when austerity measures have nobbled Greece, Marcie's Red Tractor Farm brand and sustainable business model are heaven-sent, and she might have halted the destruction of her adoptive island's ancient forests into the bargain. Now Keans have finally adopted Marcie, after 20 years' residence. But that doesn't mean they'll let her win her annual heaviest-acorn contest without putting up a fight.

Back in 2011, Marcie Mayer invited her fellow residents of Kea, an island in a shipwreck-strewn part of the Mediterranean near Athens, to a meeting about acorns. For a long time, Kea's oak trees had been in decline. This had a lot to do with the islanders finding more value in the land on which the trees stood, which could be claimed for holiday homes, and their wood, which could be repurposed as a cheap source of fuel. The oak forests that contributed so much to Kea's serene, verdant atmosphere were thinning out.

That said, there were still plenty of the trees, so each autumn, thousands of acorns would carpet the ground on farms and in back gardens, where they would just lie until they were cleared or simply merged with the ground. What else would you do with them, exactly? Well, Marcie had a few suggestions. For years she'd been researching the acorn's potential as a source of food. She'd learned how to remove the bitterness one would experience if eating them straight off the ground, how to mill them into flour, how to use that flour in cooking. The meeting was to say: Let's make Kea's oak trees part of the island's economy. Maybe that way we can save them. And by the way, what do you think of these acorn cookies? A hundred or so people attended. In a population of about 2,000 talkative people, that was more than enough. The island was informed. The harvests could begin.

Fast-forward five years. It's autumn 2016, and Marcie is in Paris, at the biennial SIAL, the biggest wholesale food fair in the world. Thanks to a combination of hard work and support from fellow islanders – plus the occasional crowdfunding experiment – Marcie has used the acorns of Kea to create a cookie business, Oakmeal, which is working out rather well. I've taken the train out to the Parc des Expositions to meet her. She guides me through

Text by Seb Emina

the show, a vast arena of Puglian cour-
gette fries, Kosovan energy drinks and
other national consumables. We arrive
at the enormous, bustling Greek zone,

then head to an area dedicated to the Oakmeal brand.
"It's like an airport," Marcie
says. SIAL is her first international exhibition, and she's hoping
to find a wholesaler for her cookies.

We take a seat. Marcie reaches into
a plastic container filled with dried
acorns and hands one over: it's dark
brown, hard and wrinkly. "All of this
didn't start with my desire to make
a cookie company," she says. "It started
with my desire to save the forest." There
is a large pack of cookies on the table.
"Try one." I pull open the vacuum seal
and am greeted by the homely aroma
of chocolate and oats. The cookies have
a thick, rough shape. I bite into one.
It is delicious, and I'm relieved that I'm
not just being polite when I tell her as
much. Because they also contain chocolate chips, vanilla and oatmeal, the
experience they offer is in many ways
a familiar one, but the acorn flour does
its part too, bringing a baritone woodi-
ness into play. She will later enter her
cookies into the Superior Taste Award
competition in Belgium. Oakmeal
will clock up the highest marks in the
biscuits/cookies category.

Marcie, who is a slim 1.73 metres,
is dressed in black except for two earrings resembling clocks ("I bought
them on eBay"). She has high cheekbones, friendly, astute eyes and one
of the catchiest laughs in the world.
She is excited to be in Paris. There
is a Magritte exhibition
at the Centre Pompidou.
She loves the Belgian sur-
realist, whose best-known painting,
"The Son of Man", is the one depict-
ing a man in front of a cloud-dotted
sky, his face obscured by a levitating
apple. "Magritte even influenced the
packaging design," Marcie says. I look
more closely at the bag, which on first
glance I had dismissed as the usual bold
commercial packaging that a budding
cookie brand must have. Now I see it:
a monochrome acorn hovering in front
of a cloudy sky, though the clouds are
fuller than the wisps in the Magritte:
they're the kind a Greek god stands on
while taking aim with a lightning bolt.

Acorn cookies: the dream of a woman
who dropped out of an art history
degree in California and ran away
to Greece. Marcie was born in 1963
and grew up in Los Altos, three miles
from Palo Alto, the city at the heart of
Silicon Valley. Her father made his fortune in weather-predicting technology;
her mother stayed home. When Marcie
was 10, a teacher named Mrs Morgan
held a class dedicated to cooking with
acorns, using "meal that we made
ourselves" – a way of learning about
California's Native American tribes,
such as the Yuruk, for whom acorns,
ubiquitous on the North American con-
tinent, have always been a staple food
source. Afterwards, Marcie tried using
acorns from the oaks near her home to
make more tasty snacks, and while she
never really managed the "tasty" part,
she also never forgot that these oval
curiosities were more than squirrel food.

Marcie made it into the University
of California, Berkeley. Then in her
final year, she took a holiday across
Greece that, strictly speaking, has yet to
finish. "That was 1984. It was supposed
to be a two-week trip, but I never left."
Marcie joined the seasonal economy,
serving food and drinks on the island of
Mykonos through the sum-
mer, retreating to Athens
in winter. Her father had
died suddenly from a heart condition in
1981, when Marcie was 17, and in 1989
she put "the last $32,000 I had from my
inheritance after college" into leasing a
restaurant in the Greek capital, bringing
Mexican food – "and the best margari-
tas in Athens" – to Psirri, now a popular
nightspot but quite different back then.

"People thought I was absolutely mad. It
was very downtrodden, but it reminded
me a lot of SoHo in New York." The
restaurant, called Blue Velvet, became
a cult success, but it was tough going,
Marcie says. "It was all done on a shoe-
string, and 16 hours a day."

In 1995, Marcie gave birth to her
only child, a daughter, Isidora, who she
has raised singlehandedly since Isidora
was eight months old. By 1997 she had
two additional branches of Blue Velvet:
a second in Athens and another on
Mykonos. But the expansion didn't go
smoothly. "I ran into all kinds of finan-
cial problems," Marcie says. "I got in
way over my head. I decided to pull out
completely. I started doing interior dec-
orating and design for shops, residences,
and especially restaurants. And that's
around the time that I went out and
rented this little cottage on the island
of Kea, right in the centre of the forest."
Located only an hour's ferry ride from
the port of Lavrio near Athens, Kea is
a convenient weekend getaway for those
who live in Greece's ancient, densely
populated capital.

She and Isidora ended up living in
that same cottage for the better part
of a decade. Marcie became fascinated
by the modest-sized valonia oaks, the
very Mediterranean *Quercus ithaburensis* subsp. *macrolepis*; they reminded her
of Mrs Morgan's cooking class. In 2005
she met a man named Kostis Maroulis,
and within six months they were married. Kostis, whose family has owned
land on Kea since the 19th century,
had inherited a farm near the harbour
town of Korissia, and in 2008 the couple turned the buildings dotted around
the land into holiday apartments. They
called the site Red Tractor Farm, after
a retired 1940s tractor – given to the
island through the Marshall Plan – that
sits near the entrance. With its productive olive grove (mostly planted by
Kostis and his father), small vineyard
and easy access to hiking routes, the
farm tends to attract online reviews that

Marcie

use turns of phrase such as "simply beautiful" and "secluded but interesting". Marcie and Kostis's relationship eventually "morphed into a business partnership," she says. He has moved elsewhere on the island, while Marcie still runs things from the two-storey house next to the guest apartments, in a complex that now includes her ever-active cookie operation. I arrange to visit in a month's time.

In the meantime, in London and Paris, curiosity takes me into four of the best-stocked health food stores I can find to see if they have acorn flour. They do not.

Kea is one of the Cyclades, a group of 220 or so islands located immediately south-east of Athens. It is both a lot like other Greek islands and completely unlike them. The surface familiarity (you will encounter delectable olive oil, melodramatic pop ballads and serene white churches filled with bright Orthodox paraphernalia) conceals a self-contained world dense with its own rituals, myths, secrets and rivalries. The island's villages were once great city-states, its ramshackle footpaths highways. Goats and sheep graze on volcanic hills split into ancient tiers. Families that have been here for centuries cross paths with Athenian holiday-homers and international tourists drawn by tales of rugged countryside, unsullied beaches, and scuba-diving visits to the wreck of the Titanic's sister ship, the Britannic, which went down nearby after an explosion in 1916.

When I arrive in Korissia, Marcie is waiting for me with her adolescent dog, Phoebe Bear, a black-haired newfypoo who leaps up and licks my face like we're old friends. (Marcie's older and calmer shepherd-collie mix, named Aise, has stayed home.) We have dinner at Rolando's, a restaurant in front of the harbour. Marcie is far more relaxed than she was at SIAL. It's the ease of someone who is, right now at this moment, in an island paradise she chose for herself. Marcie speaks fluent Greek and has been a citizen since 2009. ("It's a process I started in 1990. I had to get paperwork from all ends of the earth.") I ask if anything came out of the SIAL trip, and she tells me she's secured a Paris presence for the cookies in Galeries Lafayette.

Inevitably, we end up talking about "the crisis" – the combination of debt and refugees that has put Greece in the headlines for the past few years. On the economy, Marcie says, "It's going to take at least a decade for the pendulum to swing back, but Kea is going through it in the best possible manner. Nobody's getting rich, but everyone's surviving." As for the refugees who arrive constantly on the more southerly islands, she is in awe of the way the country has retained so much compassion. "There are still women who are cooking every day for hundreds of people."

We talk about Isidora, Marcie's daughter, who is 22 and studying psychology in the UK, in the Yorkshire city of Hull, and about how oaks were a mainstay of Kea's economy until 1965, though not as a food. Acorn caps were used in leather tanning (the term comes from the fact that hides were soaked in tannins, naturally occurring chemicals found in oaks), but when the tanneries on the mainland suddenly switched to industrial methods involving chromium sulphate, the island was left with a huge stockpile of acorn caps, and a lot of trees were felled, more or less out of sheer frustration, Marcie says.

After dinner, we drive to the farm along a dark dirt road, the stars radiant, and I go to my room, which is actually a small self-contained house at the end of a path, through a grove of 200 trees.

The next morning, Marcie shows me around the farm. We walk up a slope past networks of grapevines and arrive at a long wooden structure covered in sheets of plastic in which three tonnes of acorns are sun-drying. It's Marcie's solar table. "I found plans on the Internet from Hohenheim university in Germany. I'm trying to use as little electricity as possible." Acorns are picked across the island. A big tree can yield 200 kilograms, a medium one 60 to 100 kilograms. Compared to, say, the acorns found in a city park, by the way, the acorns of Kea are absolutely huge. Counterintuitively, this is because the drought conditions on Kea make for smaller trees, and "if a tree doesn't give its energy to itself, it gives it to its fruit or nut," Marcie says. Most of the picking is done by international volunteers. Every year Marcie offers 10 placements, for which she receives more than 1,000 applications.

Once dried, acorns can, in theory, be stored for decades. To create acorn flour, Marcie runs them through a machine that removes the shells, then soaks them to take out the bitter tannins, dries them, slices them, soaks them again, dries them once more, then mills them. The flour goes into the cookie mix, into smaller-run products such as acorn pasta, or to restaurants with particularly intrepid chefs.

The last doesn't happen too often. Acorns are so far outside the culinary mainstream that there is an actual stigma attached to eating them. Soon after Marcie told the islanders about her plans, "Older people would come up to me very quietly and very privately and tell me their individual stories about how during the Second World War they did eat them," she says. "Many people had figured out that if they put them in the fireplace and roasted them they'd be more palatable. Each person told me their story on the side, and they didn't want anybody else to know. It was the greatest shame that they'd eaten them. So after the sixth or seventh person did this, I said, 'You know, you really need to be speaking to each other because you've all eaten acorn.' Now it's kind of turned

Mayer

Καλωσορίστε στην Κέα! Marcie was photographed on her eight-acre farm in north-west Kea, Greece. As well as an orchard of oaks, the farm is home to a cannery, four small vineyards, four guesthouses and a defunct 70-year-old tractor.
Photography assistance: Christos Tzimas. Production: Boals Artists.

249

"During the Second World War, many people on Kea did eat acorns. It was their greatest shame."

The fruit of the *Quercus ithaburensis* is truly a superfood, high in protein, potassium, magnesium, calcium and vitamin B6. Every October, acorn enthusiasts are invited to stay in one of the guesthouses on Marcie's farm in exchange for 5–6 hours of acorn gathering per day.

Marcie

on its head, and people are saying, 'Well, yeah, we've been eating acorns forever.'"

But why the taboo in the first place? Is it the squirrel thing? Or the pig thing ("acorn-fed Iberico ham" being a popular fixture in the world of high-end charcuterie)? There's no similar taboo about most other foraged foods: no unease about blackberries, no blushes about mushrooms. Yet somehow the nut of the oak is seen as a food of last resort. After a talk Marcie gave on acorns was posted online, she was contacted by "end-timers", gun-and-camo types obsessed with the end of the world. What did they want, exactly? "Just to know more information, so that when the end times come they'll be ready." Pre-Armageddon, has eating acorns always been beyond the pale? Not entirely. Korea's favourite delicacies include *dotorimuk*, or acorn jelly, and *dotori guksu*, acorn noodles. Many in Turkey are partial to a hot acorn-and-vanilla drink called racahout. In Cadiz, Spain, you might be offered acorn oil in place of olive oil. Japan, Morocco, Kurdistan and Mexico all have their own acorn delicacies. Go back far enough and they were a staple right here in Greece.

 Dabbous, the Michelin-starred restaurant in Fitzrovia, London, offers a rare example of an acorn cameo in a fine-dining setting. "We use them to add an adult flavour to a savoury praline that we serve with barbecued Ibérico pork," the proprietor, Ollie Dabbous, says by email. He buys his acorn products online and values them for their nuttiness, which he says is "also great when making waffles".

By all measures, acorns should be eaten more widely. Acorns are useful. They keep you full without leaving you bloated. They are also healthy, with potassium, magnesium, flavonoids and antioxidants all present in useful quantities. Acorn flour is gluten-free, though most recipes, including Oakmeal cookies, use a combination of acorn and wheat flour. "Acorns are found on all continents of the world," Marcie says. "It could make a huge difference in world hunger if they were utilised."

Marcie's home is in no way the kind of kitsch acorn wonderland you might fear. I do spot a copy of *International Oaks: The Journal of the International Oak Society* on a bookshelf, along with perhaps every book ever published on cooking with acorns (there aren't many, though Marcie is writing her own, to be titled *Oakmeal: Essential Acorn Knowledge and Skills*). And gathered by the fireplace is a collection of acorn-themed artefacts. But most of the decor has nothing to do with acorns, and the place is really an expression of a healthy panoply of interests. Marcie is a devotee of reclaimed furniture, and almost everything in her home, including a Belgian carousel horse suspended above a door, was found and restored. "One of my regular customers at the restaurant ran up quite a bill and couldn't pay, and he said I could take something from his salvage yard." There's an old loom, one of 10 she owns, at which she weaves "utilitarian things" like table mats and beach bags, mostly with Greek cotton, which she gives away as gifts and occasionally sells. She'll teach weaving to anyone who asks.

We take a drive around the higher parts of the island, and she pulls over by a cluster of abandoned white goods, leaps out of the car, elegantly wrestles with a washing machine, and returns with the concave circle of glass from its door. "Fruit bowl," she says, handing over what is now, ripped from context, a genuinely nice piece of kitchenware.

At this time of year, the Mediterranean hill roads, with those blind corners that local drivers navigate with dodgem-like nerve, tend to be empty. Almost every time a truck or motorbike does go past, Marcie and the passing driver exchange a familiar nod or a word or two in Greek. You get the feeling it won't take long for it to be known in the villages that Marcie was travelling along this particular road at this particular time with a man in the passenger seat wearing an unsuitably large coat given the mild weather. "It took me a while to learn that when you're speaking to someone, you're not speaking to one person, you're speaking to a whole clan," she says. "You have to imagine 30 or 40 people behind them." In the case of Marcie, it's not only that everybody knows everybody. It's that this Californian in the community, an elected member of the Kea Business Association and a core member of the Kea Women's Association, is taking everybody with her on her unique journey.

"Marcie has done a great good," says professor Anastasia Pantera, a specialist in Greek agroforestry at the Technological Education Institute of Sterea Ellada, by email. "One way is the reintroduction of traditional uses of oaks that represent our natural heritage. Another is the fact that her  work helped locals financially by enhancing their income through the trade of acorns, but also through rendering Kea as an excellent example of sustainable land use and, of course, a place to visit."

Throughout her life, Marcie has experienced a string of physiological and psychological bombshells. Her father's death was just the start of it. She has multiple sclerosis, and on two separate occasions it has rendered her blind, each time for two months. She was diagnosed with breast cancer in 2009 and went through chemotherapy and a double mastectomy. That same year, her younger brother – and only sibling – died suddenly from the same condition that had killed her father. That her personality is nonetheless

Marcie

defined by lightheartedness, humour and boundless energy is quite extraordinary.

Every October, Marcie organises an acorn festival – this year's will be the seventh – a highlight of which is a competition to find and present Kea's heaviest acorn. The prize? A bottle of wine and the glow of victory, the latter of which most feasibly accounts for the genuine zeal with which triumph is pursued. Sometimes the island's gossip network brings news of dirty tricks. "I have this friend who got the clever idea to put the acorn in the fridge so it wouldn't lose weight before the competition," Marcie recalls. "I heard indirectly, and I was a bit upset about it. We had the party. It came time to weigh the acorns. I was about to hand him the wine, and this little old lady comes out of the crowd and goes [old lady voice] 'Excuse meee, I have another acorn.' And she won! *Yes!*"

The mayor of Kea, Ioannis Evangelou, is aware of my presence on the island. It would seem churlish not to pay him a visit. We drive into Ioulis, the main village – and capital of Kea – which is a cascade of white houses on a hillside in the centre of the island (the wisest place to build your capital if pirates are a concern). We trudge up a footpath to Kea's neoclassical, salmon-pink town hall. Marcie waits in reception while I meet Evangelou in his office. He is keen to increase tourism on Kea, but not if it disrupts what he calls the "tides of life". "It's remarkable, the fact that though Kea is just an hour away from the mainland, you still find people living in a very traditional way," he says. "They meet every day at noontime to have lunch together, a lunch made from produce they grow themselves." I ask him what he thinks

of my host's work. "Marcie is a pioneer," he says and smiles. "Sometimes locals have their own style of living and are suspicious about accepting an American woman showing them something new. She succeeded, and I'm very happy for that."

Pioneer: it's an interesting word. If Marcie's a pioneer, it's not in the sense of inventing something new but of reclaiming something that should never have been lost. In 2009, while going through chemotherapy, she decided to while away the hours learning to build websites. A special focus was iloveacorns.com, a repository for her interest in a nut that seemed to have been following her around since childhood. It was thanks to that website that Kea's acorns received their first spark of revived interest. An email from an interested intermediary in 2010 led to an order from a German leather tannery that still uses natural methods.

Now Marcie sells 30,000 packs of cookies per year, on the island and in mainland Europe, and employs a full-time assistant. She still acts as an unofficial broker for the acorn caps, which the German tannery still needs, and which are collected and weighed once a year. She doesn't take a profit on this, and on an island where a normal day's wage might be €40 per day, the 65 cents per kilogram one might receive for selling 2,000 kilos of acorns or caps is welcome. Recently, Marcie has also been encouraging negotiations between Kea's farmers and a family-owned factory in Turkey that turns acorn caps into a tanning agent named valex. "They can process 100 tonnes a day," she says. "It's a fantastic opportu-

nity." The oaks are becoming part of the island's identity again. Marcie has no doubt that this has slowed their destruction. If you drive inland from Red Tractor Farm, you'll spot a shop sign advertising "Acorn Products". The shopkeeper buys Marcie's flour and makes pasta and energy bars out of it, she says.

52

Evangelou would like to see the Marcie Mayer model applied to Kea's honey, figs and wine as well. In a world urgently looking for ways to be smarter with its resources, the inspiration it offers can surely go beyond the shores of one island.

The next morning, before I return to the mainland, we head into the countryside to pay a visit to the Lion of Kea, a large lichen-covered statue of a relaxing feline. It's more than 2,000 years old, and its origins have baffled many, given the lack of lions in the region.

As we carefully tread along one of the rocky pathways that cut through the hills, Marcie explains the local uses of the plants we see. "You can pickle that one... The pale green one is used as a candle wick." I ask her if she feels self-sufficient. "I've never had money, but I've also never really cared," she replies. "I grew up in an upper-middle-class family, and I had a lot of opportunities, but since then? No. But there are few times when I've wanted for something. Rather than working too many hours to afford to buy organic vegetables, I just planted the bloody garden."

42 Kea
43 Oakmeal
44 Centre Pompidou
45 Mykonos
46 HMHS Britannic, RMS Titanic
47 Newfypoo
48 Hull
49 Korea
50 Dabbous
51 International Oak Society
52 *Quercus ithaburensis*
    See Glossary on pages 344–346.

THIS

DAY

AMANDINE RENARD
SOHYUN JUNG

There's a new dynamic to everyday dressing — this look all comes down to sophisticated silhouettes and the freedom they permit. In knockout statement pieces and feminine pairings, Amandine and Sohyun bring a little extra poise to proceedings.

Photography by KARIM SADLI
Styling by JONATHAN KAYE

The asymmetrical grey-and-navy houndstooth wool coat on page 255 exhibits BALENCIAGA's tailoring ingenuity. Note the sensual sleeve of the white georgette blouse and the brilliance of the gold-and-crystal square earring and the resin-and-diamanté rectangular earring (jewellery worn throughout). All are by BALENCIAGA.

Above, the black Shetland wool jumper on the left is by DSQUARED2; on the right, the black cashmere jumper is by JASON WU.

The unmistakable grace of CÉLINE: Sohyun wears a green-and-ombre striped cotton shirt.

Opposite and overleaf, the refined beauty of a grey mohair jumper and black alpaca skirt, both by PRADA, is brought to perfection by the purple chain-motif tights and black draped pumps, both by BALENCIAGA, both worn throughout.

258

Together, this nude sheer silk top with white-and-purple varsity sleeves and the grey wool-and-silk-mix checked midi skirt create a look of urban distinction — it's CALVIN KLEIN 205W39NYC, of course.

The devastating contrast of cashmere against glittering stones: a black cashmere jumper with exposed neckline detail by JASON WU.

GUCCI's dark beige washed-gaberdine oversized trench coat with beige, wine and mustard madras-check lapels and black chevron-striped matelassé leather belt bag with brass GG logo is a coat of many details.

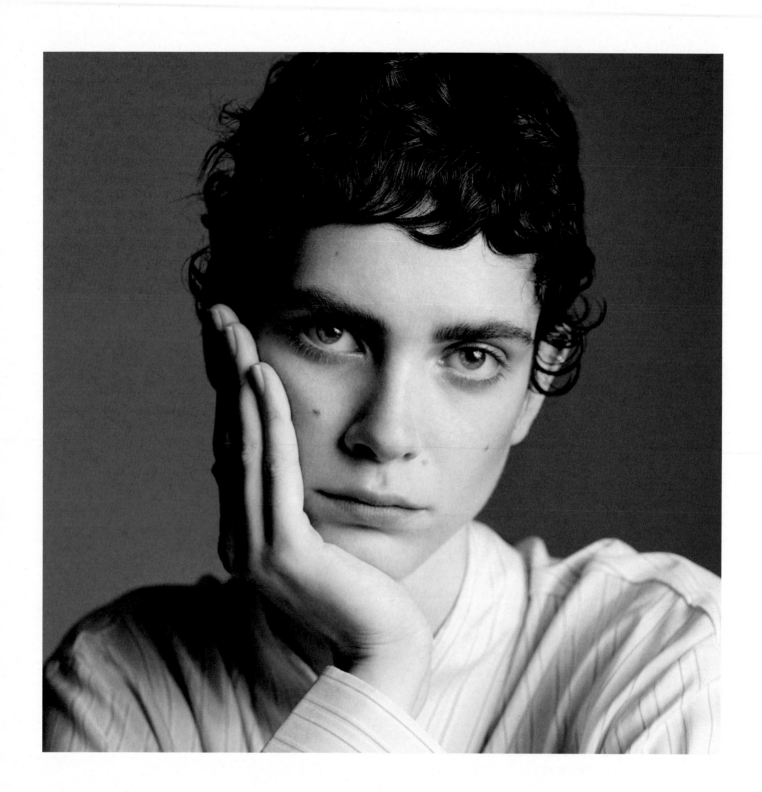

Amandine has a MULBERRY moment in a mint, cream and navy silk striped jacquard shirt by those venerable masters of quality fabrics and delicious colour.

The accent is on discreet elegance as a black wool-and-jersey-mix long-sleeved jumper by CHLOÉ is paired with softly frilled black satin trousers by GIORGIO ARMANI. The earrings are Sohyun's own.

Models: Sohyun Jung at Oui Management,
Amandine Renard at Supreme Management
Hair: Damien Boissinot at Art + Commerce
Make-up: Christelle Cocquet at Calliste Agency
Manicure: Elsa Durrens at Artlist
Set design: Alexander Bock at Streeters
Seamstress: Carole Savaton
Photographic assistance: Antoni Ciufo,
Jérôme Couderc, Chiara Vittorini
Styling assistance: Fan Hong
Hair assistance: Kyoko Kishita
Digital operation: Edouard Malfettes at DigiArt
Production: Brachfeld Paris

RAF SIMONS' black cotton double-breasted coat is one great winter essential. The addition of cosy red-and-black-striped oversized wool sleeves, also by RAF SIMONS, makes for a decisive juxtaposition.

Total: £25.98

Yana Bovenistier is wearing a pink halter top, £2.99, from MARIE CURIE; a floral lace skirt with handkerchief point hem, £5, from TRAID; and black leather biker boots, £17.99, from BARNARDO'S.

£41.96

AND
UNDER

YANA BOVENISTIER
ROSE VALENTINE

Dressing up in an expensive city can come at quite a cost. Restricting the budget — through necessity or curiosity — can recapture shopping's allure, restoring the thrill of the chase. And when the kitty is in the hands of the London-based super-thrifter Jane How, the get-ups are all the more desirable.

Photography by HARLEY WEIR
Styling by JANE HOW

Total: £26.97

remade.com

poverty out

In the window, Rose Valentine is wearing a green floral top with frill detail, £12.99; surfer print leggings, £4.99; and Vogue print platform stilettos, £8.99, all from TRAID.

Rose is wearing a Dutch wax-print dress,
£10.99, from TRAID and a black wax-
coated cotton headpiece, £12.99, from
NORTH LONDON HOSPICE. The carrier
bag was free with purchase at OXFAM.

Total: £23.83

Total: £21.98

Here and on page 278: Scotland 2007 rugby shirt, £6.95, from MARIE CURIE; brown leather trousers, £15.89, from the RSPCA; and a pink-and-white "OK" belt, 99p, from BARNARDO'S.

Orange printed flag T-shirt, £12.99, from TRINITY HOSPICE, and denim jeans, £8.99, from the BRITISH RED CROSS.

Total: £26.97

Yana is in a leopard print dress, £12.99, from TRAID; a pink nylon windbreaker, £5.99, from FARA; and blue platform stilettos, £7.99, from OXFAM. The Sainsbury's Bag for Life was free with purchase at OXFAM.

Total: £31.96

Here, Rose wears a "Fuck Cancer" T-shirt, £3.99, from CANCER RESEARCH; printed trousers, £4.99, from LONDON AIR AMBULANCE; a patchwork denim jacket, £9.99, from SHELTER; and Ugg boots, £12.99, from OXFAM.

Total: £41.96

Green-and-blue cyclist's bib shorts, £11.99, and patchwork blazer, £14.99, both from TRAID; black helmet, £9.99, from the RSPCA; and white Nike trainers, £4.99, from SHELTER.

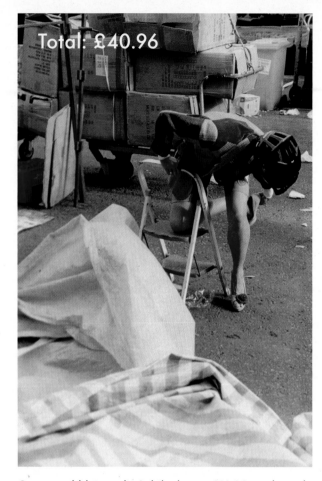

Total: £40.96

Green-and-blue cyclist's bib shorts, £11.99, and patchwork blazer, £14.99, both from TRAID; black helmet, £9.99, from the RSPCA; and cream platform shoes with bow detail, £3.99, from LONDON AIR AMBULANCE.

Total: £23.83

Total: £22.99

Yana is wearing a high-visibility-fabric
ballgown, £22.99, from TRAID. Earrings,
worn throughout, Yana's own.

279

Total: £28.97

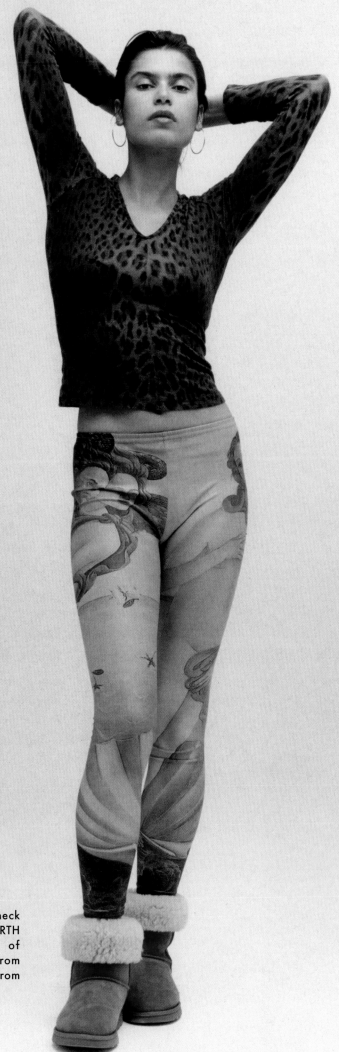

On these pages, Yana wears a V-neck leopard print top, £6.99, from NORTH LONDON HOSPICE; "The Birth of Venus" print leggings, £9.99, from TRAID; and Ugg boots, £11.99, from OXFAM. The pants are Yana's own.

Total: £18.98

Orange, white and blue tie-dye dress, £11.99, from OCTAVIA FOUN-
DATION, and multicoloured trainers, £6.99, from OXFAM.

Total: £16.99

Royal blue metallic Chanel print oversized cotton T-shirt,
£16.99, from TRAID.

Total: £28.97

Rose is wearing a green-and-white print cheongsam, £12.99; pink lace platform stilettos with bow detail, £8.99; and a Chewbacca mask, £6.99, all from TRAID.
Models: Yana Bovenistier at the Squad, Rose Valentine at Girl Mgmt. Tailor: Nafisa Tosh. Photographic assistance: Gwenaëlle C Trannoy, Jordan Lee, Pierre Lequeux. Styling assistance: Daisy Toogood, Elle Britt. Production: Art Partner.

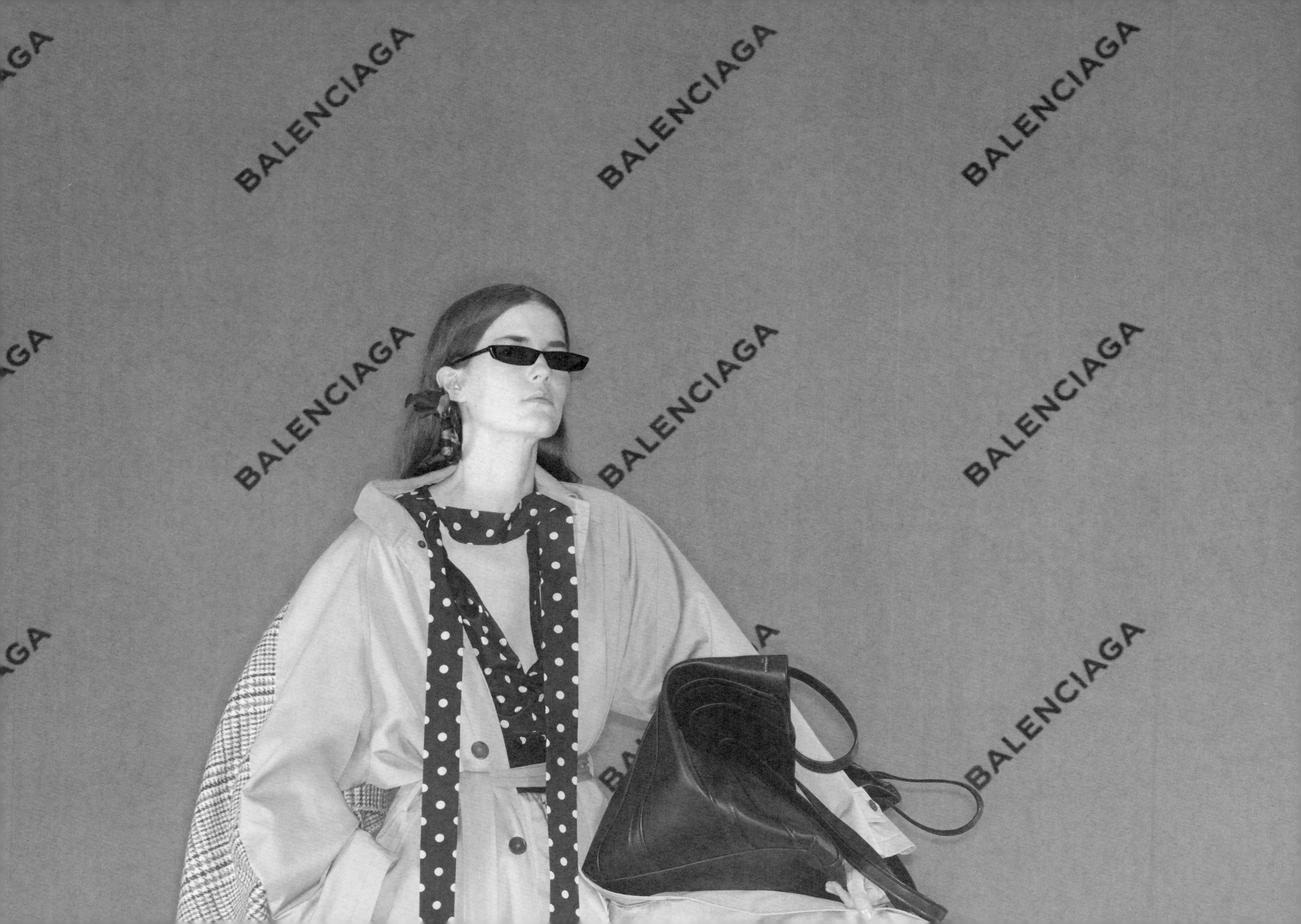

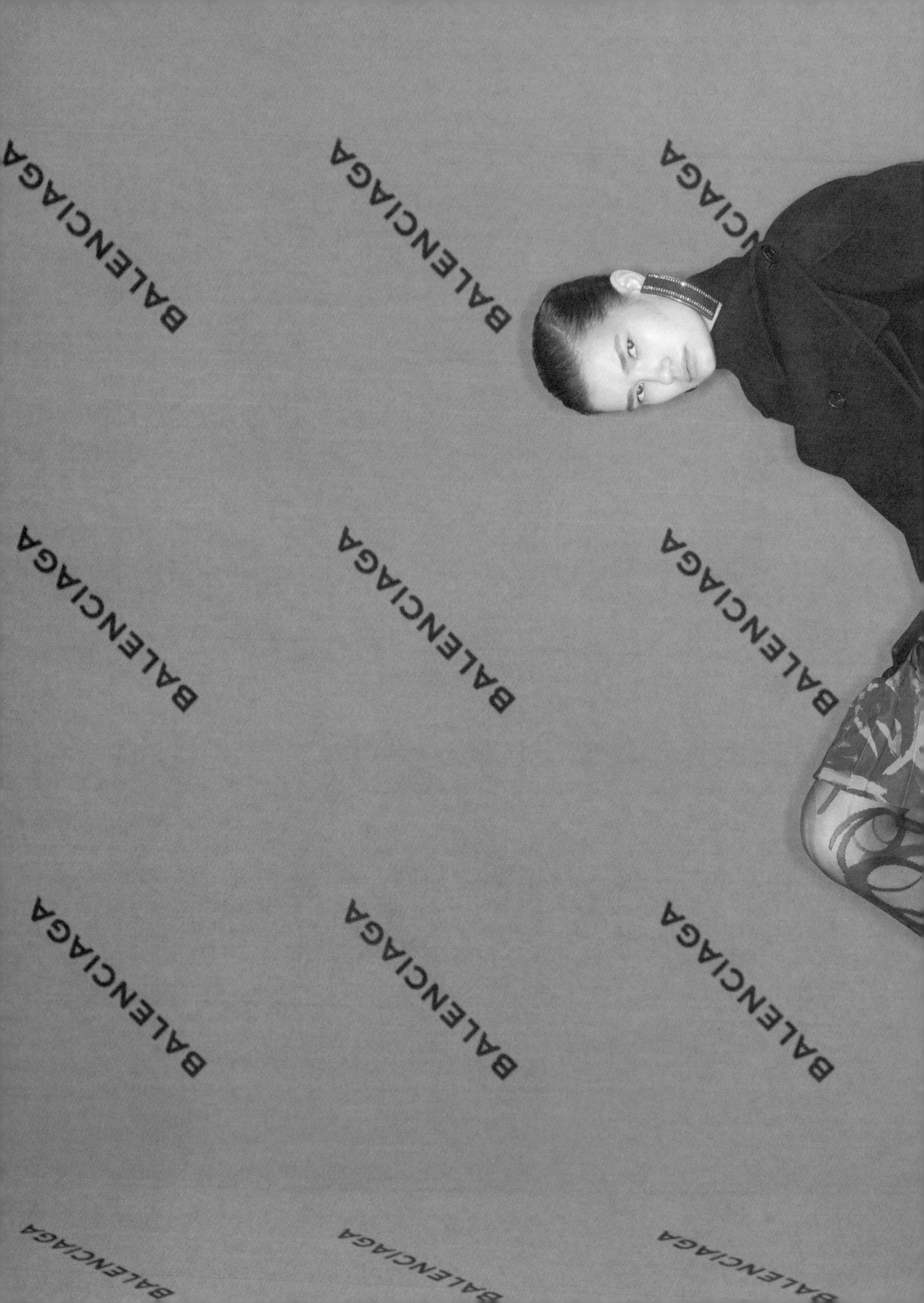
BALENCIAGA

CROS

SING

SASKIA DE BRAUW

When a ferry started running between Staten Island and New York City in 1817, the motorised boat connected the "forgotten borough" with the Battery — a gritty vestige of the 17th-century Dutch settlement of New Amsterdam. Two hundred years on, the ferry sails into a sleek district transformed by transport hubs, memorials and the fashion magazines that have migrated to Manhattan's southernmost tip. Documenting her pilgrimage to New Amsterdam in film stills here is the Dutch supermodel Saskia de Brauw, just one of the 22 million tourists and commuters who ride the ferry annually — free of charge, 24 hours a day, 365 days of each year.

Photography by ZOË GHERTNER
Styling by FRANCESCA BURNS

An all-enveloping coat is essential for windswept crossings. The black pressed-felt Sys by JOSEPH will do nicely, teamed with a wool Black Vallauris hat by JACQUEMUS. Saskia is in a vintage black polo-neck minidress over a black cotton sleeveless catsuit from DANCIA INTERNATIONAL with white cotton FALKE socks and black calf-leather Rebecca Rois shoes by CHURCH'S, all worn throughout.
On the previous page, she also wears a soft mist-coloured wool coat and trousers, both by CÉLINE.

The handsome Sys felt coat by JOSEPH and the black hat by JACQUEMUS are surprisingly versatile. Even so, the passage across the Hudson river can be rough. A good night's sleep before the trip should help to prevent seasickness, as will abstaining from alcohol before and during the journey.

This black cotton trench coat by JW ANDERSON comes with a white cotton draped collar — handy for keeping one's hair in place when necessary. Wind speeds off Staten Island can reach up to 60 miles per hour.

It only takes 25 minutes to reach Manhattan from Staten Island, but it never hurts to bring an extra layer. The sand cotton-and-wool gaberdine mac with inverted pleat is by MARGARET HOWELL, and the black faux-fur double-breasted coat with cream belt is by SIMONE ROCHA.

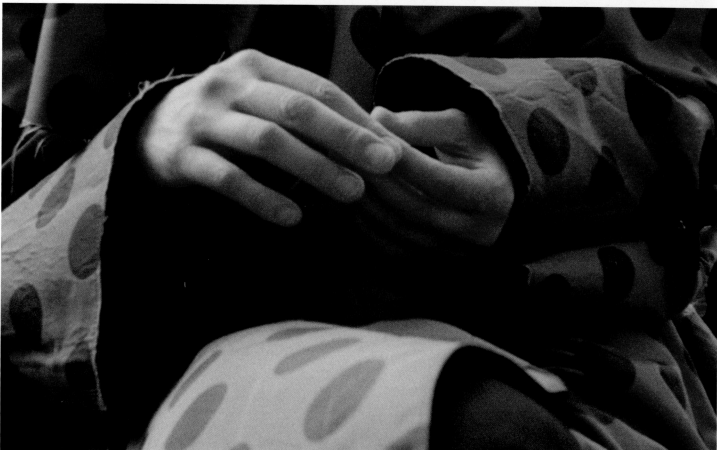

The writer George RR Martin based the kingdoms of Westeros in *Game of Thrones* on the view of Staten Island from his childhood home in New Jersey. Here Saskia looks out, wearing Dark Havana sunglasses by GIVENCHY and a dark brown-and-sand polka-dot wool-mix coatdress by LOEWE.

An arrangement of definitive outlines and complete transparency, the PVC raincoat by MIU MIU is studded with black plexi buttons.

City-bound: the double-breasted Wall Street overcoat in Glen plaid by CALVIN KLEIN 205W39NYC is from Raf Simons' debut collection for the quintessentially American brand and comes with its own smoke-coloured plastic cover.

Its silhouette showcasing the pleasingly extreme hip-to-waist ratio at the heart of the quintessential DIOR look, this full-skirted belted trench coat with epaulettes comes in navy silk.

The Staten Island Ferry has a 96 per cent punctuality rate, which means some trips last longer than others. Saskia passes the time in a navy cotton trench coat by DIANE VON FURSTENBERG.

Model: Saskia de Brauw at Viva
Model Management
Hair: Akki at Art Partner
Make-up: Fara Homidi at Frank Reps
Manicure: Alexandra Jachno
at Aim Artists Agency
Set design: Spencer Vrooman
Photographic assistance: Tucker
Vayder Wyden
Styling assistance: Claudia Alexandra
Sinclair, Molly Shillingford
Hair assistance: Rebekah Calo
Production: Connect the Dots

There's still time to make a quick change prior to disembarking at the Whitehall Terminal. Saskia adds a white cotton poplin Faubourg shirt by HERMÈS to a black wool Regent Fit suit by BROOKS BROTHERS. Smart choice.

It's possible to stay aboard all day; the Coast Guard's only stipulation is that one must get off at each terminus when sailing to and fro. Here and also on pages 302–303, Saskia sets forth once more in a full-length black wool Batavia coat with oversized collar by GIORGIO ARMANI.

SQUARES

Here, the blur of CHLOÉ's green check wool shirt coat with red buttons plays nicely with a black-and-white chequerboard T-shirt by MARQUES'ALMEIDA. The vintage tartan print leggings from BLITZ in London are worn throughout.

On page 307, it's a strident black-and-azure check wool jacket by PACO RABANNE and a purple bodysuit by FREED OF LONDON. The red nappa lace-up boots by GIORGIO ARMANI and burgundy-and-brown cotton socks by SACAI are both worn throughout. The fingerless gloves and Stewart tartan wool scarf worn throughout are from the National Theatre's costume hire department.

ELLEN DE WEER

For a category so strictly delineated, there are refreshingly few rules
when it comes to the actual wearing of checks. Jumble together as many
tartans, tattersalls and houndsteeth as you wish; it's eye-catching, yes,
but seldom ostentatious. Work a layer of colourful Lycra into the grid, and
you've got windswept-and-interesting with gymnastic dash.

Photography by THEO SION
Styling by MAX PEARMAIN

The unapologetic boxiness of the Marcia jacket typifies the season's MULBERRY collection. Here, a brown wool version with a bicolour check is worn over a vintage red, green and camel houndstooth tweed waistcoat from BEYOND RETRO.

The black-and-white houndstooth check tweed jacket and trousers are so profoundly CHANEL. They are worn with a turquoise sleeveless leotard with decorative ruching by FREED OF LONDON, a red long-sleeved bodysuit by ARABESQUE DANCEWEAR, and a red faux-fur hat by MIU MIU.

The sweeping statement atop this double-breasted BALENCIAGA creation in Prince of Wales-check wool is a near floor-length panel that's sewn into the right-hand-side darting of the coat – another thrillingly off-kilter flourish from artistic director Demna Gvasalia.

Let's go off-grid — on the right — by way of HERMÈS. This black polo-neck dress has been fronted with Les Clés-print scarf silk using the house's crafty twillaine method. The silk HERMÈS waistcoat hails from the 1980s via the STRUT ARCHIVES, London.

A sensible choice for autumn's milder months, this wool waistcoat in Prince of Wales check with mother-of-pearl buttons is by PAUL SMITH. The porcelain brooch is from a car boot sale in Chiswick (the sunglasses, too). Underneath are a green bodysuit by ARABESQUE DANCEWEAR and a sizzling all-red double whammy from GIVENCHY: a lace bodysuit with matching skirt. Brown bridle-leather shoulder bag by MARGARET HOWELL.

Cotton grey-and-white check jacket
by ERIKA CAVALLINI. Vintage screen-
printed cotton dress by LAURA ASHLEY
from the STRUT ARCHIVES. Bodysuit by
FREED OF LONDON; hat by MIU MIU.

A hint of asymmetry can disrupt the regularity of a checked look, as demonstrated by this one-shouldered wool-and-mohair LOUIS VUITTON top in navy, black and white with matching A-line skirt. It works for jewellery, too. Assorted silver bangles from PEBBLE LONDON; feathered My Boy brooch by WILLIAM & SON. Red bodysuit by ARABESQUE DANCEWEAR; navy bodysuit by FREED OF LONDON.

Big culottes? Check. This vision in navy-and-black buffalo-check wool is by DIOR. Purple sleeveless bodysuit by ARABESQUE DANCEWEAR under a pink sleeveless bodysuit by FREED OF LONDON; brooch by WILLIAM & SON.

There's more than a hint of golf-club provocateuse to these pleated tartan cashmere shorts by MONCLER GAMME ROUGE and the vintage floral tabard from STRUT ARCHIVES in London. Purple bodysuit by ARABESQUE DANCEWEAR; pink bodysuit by FREED OF LONDON; wooden bangles by PEBBLE LONDON.

Houndstooth goes hardcore with this beautifully burgundy-and-brown panelled body by SACAI. Purple bodysuit by ARABESQUE DANCEWEAR; navy bodysuit, FREED OF LONDON; bag by MARGARET HOWELL; sunglasses from a Chiswick car boot sale.

On the left, there's a pattern developing. The double-breasted burnt-sienna jacquard coat with sequin-and-bead floral appliqué and the alpaca-and-lurex geometric jacquard leggings are both by GUCCI. Turquoise leotard by FREED OF LONDON; harlequin baker-boy hat in black-and-tan leather by WALES BONNER × STEPHEN JONES MILLINERY; shoulder bag by MARGARET HOWELL; vintage porcelain brooch.

Misshapes. This asymmetrical men's cotton shirt in red-and-black tartan is by LOEWE. The white leather cape is a one-off from Portobello Road Market; the homemade label reads "By Janet". Turquoise bodysuit by FREED OF LONDON; wooden bangles by PEBBLE LONDON.

With her formative tailoring experience, STELLA McCARTNEY loves a check, as demonstrated by this handsome wool-mix shirtdress. Grey check wool waistcoat by PAUL SMITH; black bodysuit and pink bodysuit both by FREED OF LONDON; vintage BURBERRY check wool cap; vintage AQUASCUTUM house-check wool-and-cashmere scarf from ROKIT; bag by MARGARET HOWELL.

Model: Ellen De Weer at Viva Model Management. Hair: Luke Hersheson at Art + Commerce. Make-up: Hiromi Ueda at Julian Watson Agency using Chanel. Casting: Samuel Ellis Scheinman. Photographic assistance: Albi Gualtieri, Callum Toy. Styling assistance: Laura Vartiainen, Hugo Lavin, Maija Sallinen. Hair assistance: Sean Nother. Make-up assistance: Libby James, Branka Vorkapic. Production: Rep Limited.

MODEL

VILLAGE

ROSE
SARAH-JAYNE
and
SEAL

Rose Pilkington and Sarah-Jayne Todd (SJ as she's known to her intimates) just love taking off in the car with their dog, Seal. The couple's adventures in motoring have taken them from the Yorkshire coast to the Californian desert, destinations that have required the packing of everything from overcoats to T-shirts. This time, with a boot full of sumptuous seasonal separates, they headed to the sunny south-east of England to enjoy the bucolic splendour of Buckinghamshire and the wonder of Bekonscot Model Village.

Photography by COLIN DODGSON
Styling by JONATHAN KAYE

Rose, on the left, does the driving on day trips. Here, she wears a red shearling oversized pullover and silk pink, green and navy parachute pants by CHLOÉ. SJ is wearing a brown shearling bomber jacket, also by CHLOÉ, with her own jeans. In the opening spread, Rose is in a multicoloured patchwork ribbed polo-neck jumper by LOUIS VUITTON with her own jeans, while SJ is wearing a black-and-purple shrunken jumper by ARIES and her own jeans.

SJ, who is an art director, grew up in the village of Brotton in north Yorkshire, but the bright lights of the Big Smoke lured her south. On this page, she wears a glittering bubblegum-pink wool-and-lurex jacquard crew-neck jumper by GUCCI and a white cotton crew-neck T-shirt by SUNSPEL.

On the page opposite, she wears a black baby-cord bomber jacket by SAINT LAURENT by Anthony Vaccarello. The white cotton FRUIT OF THE LOOM T-shirt, black WRANGLER jeans, black VANS trainers and black cotton socks are all SJ's own.

Rose was working in a cocktail bar when the couple first met — true story. Here, she's in the red shearling jumper by CHLOÉ. SJ is wearing the brown shearling bomber jacket and a beige striped ribbed-knit jumper, both by CHLOÉ, with her own jeans, trainers and socks.

Opposite, Rose wears an umber wool brushed-knit jumper by NORSE PROJECTS with her own jeans and jewellery.

Bekonscot is the world's oldest model village, established in 1929, with a population of 3,000. As well as Minster Church, pictured here, other miniature amenities include Lee Key Plumbers' Merchants and Sam and Ella's Butchers. Just in shot is local girl Rose, who grew up in the nearby Buckinghamshire countryside.

Standing 1.73 metres tall, SJ is wearing a camel-and-black nylon parka by BALENCIAGA. The jeans, trainers and socks are her own. Rose, who is 1.80 metres, is in a yellow Double jacket and a neon green long-sleeved hooded T-shirt, both by VETEMENTS. The jeans and trainers are all Rose's own.

You may recognise SJ, 29, and Rose, 28, from the music video for the xx's ballad "Say Something Loving", released earlier this year. On the left, SJ is wearing a navy mohair jumper by DIOR. Rose, on the right, wears a green embroidered mohair beaded cardigan by PRADA.

Until SJ takes her driving test this autumn, Rose gets to have all the motoring fun. Next up, an excursion through the wilds of the Yorkshire Dales. Opposite, Rose wears a *mouliné* cashmere-cotton-mix oversized cardigan by BURBERRY — a preview of its September 2017 collection — plus a grey cotton T-shirt by CARHARTT WIP, yellow triacetate trousers by MARTINE ROSE and Rose's own trainers and socks.

Rose is wearing a burgundy Shetland wool oversized jumper by DSQUARED2 and a white cotton T-shirt by SUNSPEL. A digital artist known for her adventurous colour palettes, she has dyed her hair since she was 17 years old; she describes this tone as "peachy". We call it ravishing.

Seal is a whippet cross, and he's been Rose's loyal companion for five years — she got him when he was just eight weeks old. On the left, she is wearing a green cotton shrunken jumper by ARIES; SJ is wearing a dark blue alpaca polo-neck jumper by JOHN SMEDLEY with her own jeans.

340

So long! On the page opposite, SJ, on the left, is wearing a black polyester bomber jacket by CARHARTT WIP with her own white LEVI'S jeans; Rose wears a black cotton Melrose Place sweatshirt by A.P.C. and silk white, blue and purple parachute pants by CHLOÉ with her own trainers and socks.

Make-up: Niamh Quinn at LGA Management using Bobbi Brown. Photographic assistance: Peter Carter. Styling assistance: Fan Hong. Production: Laura Holmes Production.

A compendium of the reference images that feature in this 16th issue.

Rachel Whiteread
Pages 174–185

1

Joe Cullen of Demo One Ltd Demolition and Dismantling Engineers, operating a Fiat-Hitachi earth mover, destroyed "House" on 11 January 1994.

2

Marcus Taylor was born in Belfast in 1964. He has two artworks in Tate's collection.

3

The Brighton Wheel, also known as the Brighton O, turned three full rotations per ride which took 12 minutes. Until May 2016, that is, when it closed.

4

The Slade School of Fine Art is located on London's Gower Street, whose notable residents have included Charles Darwin and Millicent Fawcett. Until 1995, MI5 was there too.

5

"Ghost" was cast at 486 Archway Road in a house once occupied by relations of Rod Stewart. The singer was born at number 507.

6

The National Gallery of Art in Washington, DC, is one of the 19 institutions that make up the Smithsonian museums. All of them are free to visit.

7

Eric Flounders, elected in 1986, was Liberal leader of the radical Tower Hamlets borough council.

8

Phyllida Barlow was featured in The Gentlewoman Issue no° 15, photographed by Katja Rahlwes.

9

The Austrian national flag, a horizontal triband of red-white-red, was adopted in 1918 after the dissolution of the Austro-Hungarian Empire.

10

The monument opposite Whiteread's memorial in Judenplatz commemorates Gotthold Ephraim Lessing. The statue in Heldenplatz is of Prince Eugene of Savoy.

11

"Embankment", Whiteread's 2005 installation for Tate Modern's Turbine Hall, consisted of 14,000 polyethylene boxes with a total volume of 1,437 cubic metres.

12

Richard Serra is known for his giant steel sculptures; his interest in the material was sparked by watching his father in San Francisco's shipyards.

13

Every episode of the podcast S-Town ends with the song "A Rose for Emily" by the English rock-pop band the Zombies.

14

Tate's logo was designed by Wolff Olins in 2000 to give the impression it was fading in and out of focus. It was updated in 2016 by North.

15

The secret to casting in resin is not to pour too much in at once. Otherwise the mould explodes.

16

The Environmental Justice Foundation, based in Clerkenwell, London EC1, focuses on four key areas: oceans, climate, pesticides and cotton.

Laura and Kate Mulleavy
Pages 194–205

17

The Seine gets its name from Sequana, the Gallo-Roman goddess of the French river.

18

This year the University of California, Berkeley, placed sixth in Times Higher Education's ranking of the world's best universities.

19

Between 1965 and 1993, the Velvet Underground had seven line-ups, including a period in 1972–73 when the band consisted solely of Doug Yule.

20

In 2017, American Green, the first publicly traded manufacturer of cannabis products, bought the town of Nipton in north-east California for $5 million with the intention of transforming it into a marijuana-friendly tourist resort.

21

London's Design Museum nominated Rodarte's *Star Wars*-inspired Death Star dress from A/W '14 for its 2015 Designs of the Year awards.

22

Woodshock also stars the actor Pilou Asbæk.

23

Rodarte's logo is a custom design by Li, Inc., based on the font Nimbus Roman No 9 Condensed Bold.

24

Those Mulleavys do enjoy a pun: other logo variations featured on Rodarte's popular line of cotton casuals are Rosarte and Rohearte.

25

The Lost Boys was shot in Santa Cruz, — it became Santa Carla ("Murder Capital of the World") in the film so as not to destroy the local tourist trade.

Simone Biles
Pages 210–223

26

Simoji by Simone Biles features 55 emoji stickers.

27

The "Final Five" — Simone Biles, Gabby Douglas, Laurie Hernandez, Madison Kocian and Aly Raisman — chose their nickname to reflect that teams will be reduced to four gymnasts for Tokyo 2020.

28

Alicia Garza of Black Lives Matter coined the phrase on 13 July 2013, the day neighbourhood watch volunteer George Zimmerman was acquitted of the murder of Trayvon Martin.

29

The actor Rosie Perez was nominated for three Emmys for her work as the choreographer for *In Living Color*'s in-house dance troupe, the Fly Girls.

30

The scoreboard at the Montreal Olympics had not been programmed for a perfect 10. When Romanian Nadia Comăneci was awarded the first one on 18 July 1976, it came up as a score of 1.00.

31

"Vault" or "VT" as it is abbreviated in gymnastics for scoring purposes, is both a noun and a verb as Simone demonstrated exuberantly here in Rio.

32

The American governing body has 148,000 members. Its motto is "Begin Here, Go Anywhere."

33

Ron Biles has been a Nina Simone fan since his teens and suggested that his daughter name his then granddaughter after the singer.

34

The International Gymnastics Federation is the world's oldest international sports organisation. It was founded on 23 July 1881.

35

Simone has 3.5 million followers on Instagram and 970,000 on Twitter.

36

Simone and Sasha Farber received the judges' top score of 40 for their final performance on *Dancing with the Stars* — a jive to "Faith" by Stevie Wonder.

37

The motto on the Belizean flag is "Sub Embra Floreo", meaning "Under the shade I flourish".

Martine Rose
Pages 236–243

38

The MTV logotype, of which Martine Rose's is a version, was created by Pat Gorman, Frank Olinsky and Patty Rogoff of Manhattan Design in 1981.

39

BOY, at 153 King's Road, was raided by police on the day it opened in 1977. It is said that tourists were scared to enter for fear of being spat on.

40

If Jeff Goldblum hadn't gone into acting, he would have followed his passion for music; the *Jurassic Park* star is an accomplished jazz pianist.

41

Martine Rose presented her 27-look Spring/Summer 2018 collection on 11 June 2017.

Marcie Mayer
Pages 244–252

42

The Greek lyric poet Simonides was born on Kea in 556 BC. He invented the letters η, ξ, ψ and ω. He was also considered a greedy miser.

43

It's not just Oakmeal that pays homage to "The Son of Man"; the painting is also referenced in Michael Jackson's video for "Scream".

44

Until 1997, 20 per cent of visitors to the Centre Pompidou just took the escalators up the outside of the building — bypassing the ticket booth completely.

45

ΜΥΚΟΝΟΣ

The vibrant Greek island of Mykonos is located at 37.4467° N, 25.3289° E.

46

HMHS Britannic (1915) and RMS Titanic (1912) were two of the three ocean liners built for White Star Line; the third was RMS Olympic (1911). All sank.

47

Intelligent and affectionate, the newfypoo breed requires moderate exercise and regular grooming.

48

Hull's most amazing resident was probably Mick Ronson, though a former librarian of its university, Philip Larkin, comes a close second.

49

During the Vietnam War, President Park Chung-hee asked Lyndon B Johnson to ensure kimchi reached Korean troops—it was "vitally important for morale".

50

In a 2012 review, the late critic AA Gill described Dabbous's food as "close to perfect".

51

International Oak Society members receive the Oak News & Notes newsletter twice a year.

52

"Tie a Yellow Ribbon Round the Ole Oak Tree" by Dawn sold three million records in the US in three weeks in 1973.

A complete compendium of the brands featured in this magazine together with their websites.

3.1 Phillip Lim 31philliplim.com
A.P.C. .... apc.fr
Adidas .... adidas.co.uk
AG Jeans .... agjeans.com
Alaïa .... alaia.fr
Alexander McQueen ..... alexandermcqueen.com
Arabesque Dancewear
.... dancewear-arabesque.co.uk
Aries .... ariesarise.com
Balenciaga .... balenciaga.com
Battenwear .... battenwear.com
Beautiful People ... beautifulpeoplecollection.com
Beyond Retro .... beyondretro.com
The Big Pause .... thebigpause.co.uk
Birkenstock .... birkenstock.com
Blitz .... projectblitz.com
Brooks Brothers .... brooksbrothers.com
Burberry .... burberry.com
By Malene Birger .... bymalenebirger.com
Calvin Klein 205W39NYC .... calvinklein.com
Carhartt WIP .... carhartt-wip.com
Cartier .... cartier.co.uk
Catbird .... catbirdnyc.com
Céline .... celine.com
Chanel .... chanel.com
Chloé .... chloe.com
Christopher Kane .... christopherkane.com
Church's .... church-footwear.com
Contemporary Wardrobe ....
.... contemporarywardrobe.com
COS .... cosstores.com
Dancia International .... dancia.co.uk
Delfina Delettrez .... delfinadelettrez.com
Diane von Furstenberg .... dvf.com
Dickies .... dickiesworkwear.com
Dion Lee .... dionlee.com
Dior .... dior.com
Dries Van Noten .... driesvannoten.be
Dsquared2 .... dsquared2.com
Erika Cavallini .... erikacavallini.com
Falke .... falke.com
FitFlop .... fitflop.com
Freed of London .... freedoflondon.com
Giorgio Armani .... armani.com
Givenchy .... givenchy.com
Gucci .... gucci.com
Hermès .... uk.hermes.com
Jacquemus .... jacquemus.com
Jason Wu .... jasonwustudio.com
Jil Sander .... store.jilsander.com
John Lobb .... johnlobbltd.co.uk
John Smedley .... johnsmedley.com
Joseph .... joseph-fashion.com

JW Anderson .... j-w-anderson.com
Kate Spade New York .... katespade.co.uk
Kvadrat .... kvadrat.dk
L.L. Bean .... global.llbean.com
Lanvin .... lanvin.com
Lee .... lee.com
Levi's .... levi.com
Loewe .... loewe.com
Louis Vuitton .... louisvuitton.com
Margaret Howell .... margarethowell.com
Marques'Almeida .... marquesalmeida.com
Martine Rose .... martine-rose.com
MHL .... margarethowell.co.uk
Miu Miu .... miumiu.com
MM6 Maison Margiela ...... maisonmargiela.com
Moncler .... moncler.com
MSGM .... msgm.it
Mulberry .... mulberry.com
Mystery Ranch .... mysteryranch.com
Nehera .... nehera.com
Nike .... nike.com
Norse Projects .... norseprojects.com
Paco Rabanne .... pacorabanne.com
Paul Smith .... paulsmith.com
Pebble London .... pebblelondon.com
Philosophy di Lorenzo Serafini ....
.... albertaferretti.com
Polo Ralph Lauren .... ralphlauren.co.uk
Ports 1961 .... ports1961.com
Prada .... prada.com
Proenza Schouler .... proenzaschouler.com
Pucci .... emiliopucci.com
Raf Simons .... rafsimons.com
Repossi .... repossi.com
Rodarte .... rodarte.net
Rokit .... rokit.co.uk
Roksanda .... roksanda.com
Ruco Line .... rucoline.com
Sacai .... sacai.jp
Saint Laurent .... ysl.com
Santoni .... santonishoes.com
Simone Rocha .... simonerocha.com
Sonia Rykiel .... soniarykiel.com
Sportmax .... sportmax.com
Stella McCartney .... stellamccartney.com
Stuart Weitzman .... stuartweitzman.com
Sunspel .... sunspel.com
Strut Archives .... strutlondon.tumblr.com
Toast .... toa.st/uk
Toga .... toga.jp
Tokyo Lab .... tokyolab.co.uk
Topshop .... topshop.com
Vetements .... vetementswebsite.com
Vince .... vince.com
Wales Bonner .... walesbonner.net
William & Son .... williamandson.com

Photography by Zoë Ghertner, styling by Francesca Burns.

A final word.

Though everything has been said for now in this printed instalment of the magazine, the particularly
curious can sign up for further entertainment and notification by joining The Gentlewoman Club. Until February 2018,
that is, when we'll be back with a 17th issue. Farewell for now, readers!